GOD IS YOUR
MATCHMAKER

GOD IS YOUR MATCHMAKER

STEPHANIE HERZOG

DESTINY IMAGE® PUBLISHERS, INC.

P.O. Box 310, Shippensburg, PA 17257-0310

"Speaking to the Purposes of God for this Generation and for the Generations to Come."

This book and all other Destiny Image, Revival Press, Mercy Place, Fresh Bread, Destiny Image Fiction, and Treasure House books are available at Christian bookstores and distributors worldwide.

For a U.S. bookstore nearest you, call 1-800-722-6774.

For more information on foreign distributors, call 717-532-3040.

Reach us on the Internet at www.destinyimage.com.

ISBN 10: 0-7684-2720-7
ISBN 13: 978-0-7684-2720-2

For Worldwide Distribution, Printed in the U.S.A.

2 3 4 5 6 7 8 9 10 / 12 11 10 09

DEDICATION

First and foremost, I dedicate this book to my three daughters, whom I love with an everlasting love. May they learn, above all else, how to live out their singleness for God and receive their identity and fulfillment solely from Him. If the Lord wills that they each marry, may they trust Him to choose only the best man for His divine purpose.

Finally, to all who are single in the family of God, may you take pleasure in and prefer God's ways and standards in finding fulfillment and true happiness in life. I pray that you let God choose His best for you and for what He has planned for your life. I guarantee that you will never regret it, regardless of the trials and pressures you go through. By doing things God's way, you will see that your future is greater and brighter than your past and present.

ACKNOWLEDGMENTS

Thank you, heavenly Father, for Your love, goodness, guidance, faithfulness, and most of all, for fathering me throughout my entire life. Thank You for loving me before I ever loved You and for making me part of Your precious royal family. Your wonderful principles and ways that You tenderly and lovingly instilled into my life have brought great treasures beyond what I could ever imagine. Thank You for the honor and privilege of being a conduit of Your love, inspiration, and wisdom to the singles who will read this book. May their hearts be open to Your truth, Your ways, and Your blessings as they discover that the only key to true happiness, life, and fulfillment is having a real and deep intimate love relationship with You.

Great thanks to David Herzog—whom God chose and gave to me as His most precious and perfect gift, my dearest husband, my partner in life, my encourager, the greatest male cheerleader and supporter, my best friend throughout life's journey and trials, and next to God, the greatest love of my life. David, I enjoyed writing my book simultaneously as you wrote yours—*The Ancient Portals of Heaven*. I will never forget the long nights spent writing our books together until we dropped, helping each other out, praying together, and birthing together things in the Spirit for what has now come to be finished products. I enjoyed the little breaks in the wee hours of the night, although I think you took way more breaks for snacks than I did. What an unforgettable and amazing experience! Always remember that, even after almost 17 years of marriage, you still rock my world! Thank you for your ever-increasing love for me, for believing in me, and for encouraging me to write and finish this book.

To Dawn Scott, a precious friend and powerful minister along with her husband, Randy, from Denver, Colorado. I am so glad that an awesome outpouring of the Holy Spirit broke out when we were at your place. David, the children, and I cherish and love you and your family. Thank you so much for all of your help in proofreading the book in the middle of revival. You are such a great blessing!

To Megan Allison for providing me the feedback that I needed and for believing in the message and the messenger of this book. It encourages me to see singles like you going all the way with God, living your singleness according to His standards, and enjoying it. May many more singles learn to enjoy a completely fulfilled singleness as you do.

To Olivia Pearce for taking great care of my babies, the house, and the ministry, especially during the writing of this book. Your help allowed me to fully concentrate on my writing. Seeing my precious girls under your care gave me such peace and joy because I knew they were in good hands. Thank you for your great service.

To Dennis Trout for the wisdom shared in his *Against the Grain* manual. His knowledge on the subject of dating truly exposes dating for what it really is.

To Dr. Don Raunikar and his book *Choosing God's Best*, which confirmed many of the concepts and principles that are the foundation of my beliefs regarding dating.

TABLE OF CONTENTS

FOREWORD

Transparency and honesty! Wisdom and counsel! *God is Your Matchmaker* is a book every single and married person should be required to read! There is a crisis in the Body of Christ concerning relationships among singles and married people. Outside of salvation, marriage is the next most important decision anyone makes in their life, and yet so little is written about it.

Stephanie Herzog has lived this message, so she is well qualified and equipped to share many golden nuggets of wisdom and truth, coupled with the Word of God, to expose "blind spots" and flawed thinking in the Body of Christ. She dismantles belief systems and lies of the enemy with candor and conviction, revealing the pitfalls and traps the enemy uses to ensnare singles with tolerance and compromise. These traps carry over into marriages—sadly causing as many divorces between believers as nonbelievers.

GOD IS YOUR MATCHMAKER

This is a "how to" guide to receiving God's *best* for your life, using godly principles as a plumb line along with the Word and the Lord's heart as you walk out your singleness or prepare for marriage.

Jill Austin
President and Founder, Master Potter Ministries
National and international conference speaker and author
info@masterpotter.com
www.masterpotter.com

INTRODUCTION

Dear friend, it is neither by accident nor by chance that you are holding this book in your hands. Reading what I have to say may have the impact of a bright light illuminating a dark room. At first the bright light almost blinds you, but eventually your eyes adjust, and you realize that you can actually find your way around the room as your capacity to see increases. Though your eyes may have adjusted to the darkness, the available light illuminates many details that you could not previously see. You begin to notice the very things that caused you to stumble and fall, the garbage that has been in your life for years. Finally you see it for what it really is and can eliminate it.

It is not the purpose of this book to give you tips about how to "catch" a man or a woman. I believe that is a complete waste of time and runs counter to God's design for relationships. This book is intended to take you to a different place in God that will revolutionize your preconceived ideas about singleness and marriage, and it deals truthfully with these issues. These principles may seem unfamiliar at first because they are not commonly taught. Therefore I challenge you to look deeper into allowing God to be your matchmaker.

My heart is to help you understand that singleness is just as much a gift from God as marriage. The apostle Paul said, *"But I wish everyone were single, just as I am. But God gives to some the gift of marriage, and to others the gift of singleness"* (1 Cor. 7:7 NLT). Neither one is better or worse than the other. What is ironic is that often single people want to be married and married people want to be single again. Both seasons in life have their own share of joys, advantages, responsibilities, struggles, and pain. Marriage is not a promotion from singleness. Don't miss the joy you can have today just because you think singles are less deserving.

In my travels throughout the United States and other nations, I have observed three categories of singles among Christians:

1. Those who believe they are an incomplete person if not married.

2. Those who are strong and active in the Lord, yet are totally clueless regarding the dynamics of personal relationships.

3. Those who choose God's way and will never be sorry or face lives of regret.

Unfortunately, the largest and most common group consists of those who think they are incomplete or that something is wrong with them because they are single. They feel frustrated and depressed, which can lead them easily into making two errors—entering into a wrong relationship out of desperation or continuing to live in prolonged depression and frustration. These errors in judgment can lead to rebellion against God rising from the feeling that God is punishing them or being unfair.

They wonder: *Why is everyone getting married but me? What if I never marry? What is wrong with me that no one wants to marry me?* These questions and doubts permeate everyday life with tremendous emotional force such as fear, worry, grief, jealousy, frustration, anger, self-pity, depression, and rejection.

Some singles put their lives on hold waiting for a mate, assuming that they cannot lead a productive and fulfilling life, or even serve God effectively, until they are married. This is a dangerous misconception that runs completely counter to the counsel of Scripture. Don't wait for your mate before obeying God and fulfilling His destiny for you. Postponing your response to God's call just because you don't have a partner alongside of you leads only to a frustrating and fruitless life. Embracing that purpose now, however, and deciding to be in the center of God's will and to follow Him with your whole heart, even while you are single, will bring true peace, contentment, and fulfillment to your soul.

Simply being a born-again believer is not enough to ensure success in this area, which brings me to the second category of singles. These singles are fired up for God, strong in the Lord, and active in His service, yet they are totally clueless and lacking in godly wisdom and knowledge regarding the dynamics of personal relationships. They use the same approach as the secular world and end up in relationships with people they were not meant to be with. I have not encountered many churches that teach biblical principles regarding dating anymore. Therefore it is no surprise when Christian relationships have results similar to the world's relationships.

Then there are the faithful few who fall into the third category of singles who choose God's way and will never be sorry or face a life of regret. They are confident and secure in who they are in Christ, and they do not need a mate to make them feel complete. They focus more on their calling and how to fulfill it than on their singleness.

My goal is to help you find fulfillment in your singleness in God by knowing His way. If you can learn to trust God with your present, and witness His day-by-day faithfulness, you will find it much easier to trust Him with your future. God has everything under control. Nothing escapes Him. Be assured of this: whatever He has for you, whether a prolonged singleness or a soon-to-be marriage, it is all part of His perfect will and plan for your life—the only plan that will bring you true joy, fulfillment, and fruitfulness.

The only way to find the right person is to know first of all that you are on the right path with God, living in the center of His perfect will for you. His blessings and gifts are only found in the center of His will. You won't find Mr. or Ms. Right on "Wrong Avenue." A wrong turn will never take you to where you want to be. Make sure you are right where God wants you to be. Once you are on the right track, you will realize that the Lord Himself is the only Person you truly need. Everything and everyone else fall short next to Him. He is the only One who can complete you.

Introduction

Who better than our God and Creator knows what we truly need? And who could have our best interests at heart more than the One who loves us enough to send His own Son to die for us so that He might draw us into a love relationship with Him? God is and always will be our perfect Guide and Matchmaker. Unlike the world, His ways and His love never change. He stays the same.

God is raising the bar. The standard He has established for marriage is high but not unattainable. There are Christians worldwide, from different races and backgrounds, who can testify that God's plan works. Any Christian willing to meet God's conditions can experience its outworking in his or her own life. I can truly say with complete confidence and certainty that my husband, David, is God's chosen one for me—His perfect will, and His best gift to me. And David says the same about me. Sadly, not every married person can say that with absolute certainty and confidence, especially when caught in the middle of a crisis that fuels worry and doubt or when feeling overwhelmed with mundane affairs and responsibilities that have squelched all sense of romance from the marriage.

As Paul wrote in First Corinthians 7:7, singleness and marriage both are gifts from God. This means that He is the One who does the choosing and the giving. It is not for us to choose on our own and then seek God's stamp of approval. With marriage, as with all stages or seasons of life, we do not need to adopt Hollywood's false portrayal of life. Instead we need to seek the mind of Christ to ensure that we do not take the wrong path or make the wrong choices.

Next to salvation, no decision we make in life is more important than the decision about who to marry. That decision will forever change our world, affecting not only our future, but also the lives of generations yet unborn. For this reason, we dare not take it flippantly or be careless about it. Marriage is a holy covenant and commitment. As God's children, we should want a godly and blessed marriage, above and beyond what the world has ever seen and known. Let us do it God's way all the way, without any mixture with the world.

I pray that you will open your heart to what God has to say concerning your life as a single, whether marriage is part of it or not. If marriage is to be part of your future, let God supernaturally bring you together, just as He brought David and me together. Throughout the book, I will carefully point out false principles and counter them with God's principles concerning this subject. God's principles for marriage are revealed in His Word. Although the application of these principles may be different for each person because each situation is different, God's principles stay the same.

As His child, you are entitled to His very best. Don't settle for anything less. You are His responsibility. Trust Him completely, and He will open every door of His will to you. He will fulfill every plan and purpose that He has for your life. But as His child, remember also that from now on you do not make your own decisions apart from Him. We all have free will, but when we yield and submit our will to God's, His will becomes our will and His choices our choices. *God gives His very best to those who leave the choice up to Him.*

Jeremiah 29:11 teaches us that *God's plans for us are for good and not to bring harm to us because He loves us.* Few of His children truly comprehend what this means. The enemy works hard to keep the children of God blinded to His love, which causes them to not trust the heavenly Father (with their future) and, therefore, miss out on obtaining His very best for them.

If marriage is part of God's plan for you, then you can trust Him to work out every detail, both for you and for the mate He has destined for you. Without any effort on your part—without you trying to "make things happen"—He will bring you together with a person who is exactly suited to you. In this way, the two of you may experience marriage as God originally designed it, a relationship on a much higher level than the world has ever dreamed of.

But if marriage is not part of God's plan for you, He will give you the strength and the grace to live in singleness *fully satisfied.* He will show you how He wants you to use your singleness for His glory and how you can be fulfilled in it. Don't let your singleness be wasted. *"If people can't see what God is doing [in their lives], they stumble all over themselves; but when they attend to what He reveals, they are most blessed"* (Prov. 29:18 TM). Find out God's plan for your life as a single, live it out faithfully, and you won't stumble and die in the wilderness.

Whatever God's plan for you may be—married or single—rest assured that it is for your best and that in that plan you will find your greatest fulfillment, contentment, and fruitfulness. Think of this book not as a rulebook for personal happiness but as a guidebook to help you find your way to God's best so that you can be eternally blessed.

chapter 1

MY LIFE AS A SINGLE

My mother was already a born-again Christian, but not Spirit-filled, when she married my father, a nominal and non-practicing Catholic. She was never taught that God does not want His children to marry non-Christians, so out of ignorance, she married my dad. Consequently, they didn't share the same values and principles about how to raise a family. Even though it was done in ignorance, this "unequal yoking" (see 2 Cor. 6:14) did not spare her from suffering terrible consequences in her marriage and family.

When I was 6 years old, I gave my life to Jesus during Sunday school. My life was forever changed as I got to know Jesus not only as my Lord and Savior but also as my closest friend and Father. He became so real to me that I could talk to Him and He would talk back to me. I felt His presence whenever I worshiped Him and even when I just thought about Him. Even as a young child, I hungered and thirsted for more of Him. I constantly asked Mom to read the Bible to me and teach me more of Him.

My dad went to church with my mom every Sunday, but for social reasons. He didn't want to surrender his life completely to Jesus, but he enjoyed the people who went to church. Church to him was like a nice social club. Dad had a hard time showing love and affection to his family. The only type of communication he knew how to give was negative. He thought that criticizing us, putting us down, and comparing us with other kids would shame us into automatically doing what was right and showing him honor and respect. He called it reverse psychology. Since he served in the U.S. Navy for a few years, he adapted their sailors' training program to raise his children. He forgot that we weren't sailors being trained for war but children who needed love, attention, encouragement, approbation, and loving admonition. He also believed that the best way to get his children to respect him was by using fear and intimidation—what he got was the opposite. You can't expect to reap a positive harvest when only negative seeds are sown.

My older sister believed what my father said about her and she became a rebel. All she really wanted and needed was love, positive attention, and approbation. So for her, negative attention was better than none at all. My younger brothers believed him too, and this negative upbringing caused them a lot of emotional damage, harming their ability and motivation to finish or succeed in anything. They expressed their pain and their cry for love in different ways: one suffered from deep depression and self-inflicted mental problems, while the other got involved with drugs, pornography, and bad relationships.

I, on the other hand, responded differently. I wanted to prove to my dad that he was wrong and that I was smart and would succeed in life because of God and the love that I received from Him the moment He came into my life. Without the love and saving grace of God, when I gave my heart to Jesus, who knows how I would have turned out. I owe everything to Him. His presence in my life helped me develop a positive attitude that enabled me to excel in school and win many awards.

As a child, I asked God, *Father, since my earthly dad has a difficult time giving me the love and encouragement I need as a child, will You father me?* I asked God to teach me His ways (what was right and wrong), to love me, to approve of me, to encourage me, to guide me, to be supportive of me, to make me feel safe and secure, to reassure me that everything would be all right—basically all of the things an earthly father ought to do. And He surely did.

I remember crying many times in the night, as a teenager, and giving over to the Lord all the hurt I felt from my dad. In return, God always filled me with His love and comfort. Sometimes I could feel His love tangibly, almost like He was literally holding and hugging me. By the time morning came, the joy of the Lord filled my heart, and I would go to school with joy flowing out of me. I was even known in my school as someone who was cheery and always had a smile.

ME? HOMECOMING QUEEN?

By letting God father me, I was spared a major identity crisis that I might have had otherwise. Like every teenager growing up,

I had to deal with some issues of rejection and insecurity. Every time I ran to God with them, He was faithful to bring light and healing. Growing up, I had no difficulty complimenting others, but because I was so accustomed to hearing only negative things about myself at home, I had difficulty accepting compliments and affirmation from others, except from God. Whenever people said something nice about me, I thought they either were lying or kidding. I was taught to believe that, if I accepted compliments, I would become prideful. By refusing them, I would be walking in humility.

God had to heal that area of my life. He showed me that by refusing the compliments of others, I was actually walking in false humility—the kind that God does not accept. Since *He* thought greatly of me, whenever others saw and acknowledged my good qualities, I should receive them with a simple, "Thank you," with no embarrassment or shame. It took me a long time to fully accept that, but I'm glad the Lord was patient and never gave up on me.

During my senior year in high school, the Lord showed me what He really thought of me by allowing me to become homecoming queen. My friends turned in my picture without my knowledge and encouraged others to vote for me. I didn't think I would win because of the other more beautiful "Barbie" girls who were in the competition. The night before Homecoming, I went to bed crying my eyes out because my dad had said some horrible and cutting things to me even though I had done nothing wrong. I went to school the next day with puffy eyes and very low self-esteem. I was so distracted by my own hurt that when the winners were being announced, I didn't even hear my name. My friend sitting next to me said, "Hey Steph, didn't you hear your name? They've called you at least three times. You better get up there!"

At first I didn't believe it, but as I listened for myself, I realized it was true! Absolutely awestruck, I hesitantly worked my way up to the stage. Out of 30 girls, there were three finalists—and I was shocked to be one of them. Surely there had been a mistake. Surely there were others who were prettier. It finally began to sink in that I had won when they handed me a huge bouquet of roses.

When I got home that afternoon and explained to my mother that I had been chosen homecoming queen, she was so happy and excited and gave me a big hug and kiss. When my dad finally got home, he saw the roses and asked where they came from. When my mom told him, all he said was, "Oh, they probably fixed who was going to win." He just couldn't bring himself to believe that I had really won fair and square and that something as special as that could happen to me. It was as though he didn't want to see me happy, preferring to see me sad and miserable. What a blow that was to me.

But my heavenly Daddy was quick to tell me what He thought as He said, *Don't mind what he just said to you. It doesn't matter if that's how he sees it. I see you as My princess, and to Me, you are the most beautiful and deserving of the title. I am the King of kings, and you are My daughter; that makes you royalty, and no one can take that from you.* I was comforted by His words and cherished them forever.

MY DATING EXPERIENCE

In junior high, boys liked me, but I didn't know how to respond or how to handle such situations. Since my parents didn't sit with me and explain these things, I learned mainly from watching television, movies, and my Christian relatives. According to them, dating was OK. Even though I had both Christian and non-Christian friends who dated, I didn't feel a need to do the same. For me, Jesus was sufficient. He constantly filled me up, and I felt no need for anyone else.

When I finally reached high school, more boys paid attention to me, and I began to like them as well. I knew I needed some guidance about how to go about it the right way, so I asked a Christian cousin of mine for advice. She said that dating was normal for a teenager. My aunt and uncle both approved of it, so I started dating. If only I had known then what I know now—I would not have dated at all. I could have avoided a lot of wasted time, emotions, and energy.

After dating casually a couple of times, I learned to give boys a hard time. I was very direct and told them straight up that I was a Christian and that they couldn't have sex with me or mess around with me in any way. Right away I explained my standards. If a guy still wanted to go out with me, I always suggested going to my church or youth group. I preserved my virginity and guarded it seriously. I made up my mind not to give that away to anybody except my husband, as my gift to him.

Because of my high standards, my dating relationships never

lasted very long. The longest was four weeks. I didn't date much by choice because I found it to be a waste of time and emotions. I experienced both how to break a boy's heart and how it felt to have my own heart broken. Eventually I got so sick and tired of it that I took the whole matter to God. I was certain He had a better way of putting two people together than dating like the world. I also knew that, as a teenager, I could redirect all of my energy and passion to something better that would build God's Kingdom instead of wasting it on boys.

PRAYING FOR MY FUTURE HUSBAND

When I was about 17 years old, my mother advised me to start praying for my future husband. I didn't understand how I could pray for someone I didn't know yet, but she simply explained that I could ask God to preserve him for me and to deliver him from every temptation, and that I could pray that he would be one who was already following God and walking in righteousness. I told her, "Oh, in that case, I can do that. I'm sure God can tell me more things to pray about as I do it everyday. And if I run out of things to pray, I can always pray in the Spirit for Him to help him in situations that only God would know." And so I did exactly that.

Then one day I told my mom, "Since I'm saving myself for my future husband and preserving my virginity just for him, he'd better do the same thing for me. I don't see in the Bible where only girls should be virgins and guys get to do whatever they want. I believe that both Christian girls and boys need to preserve their virginity and purity until they get married, no exceptions. And so I have decided that my future husband will be a virgin like me when we get married."

My mother replied, "Oh Stephanie, nowadays, it's very rare to find a virgin man to marry. There are maybe only two percent left who are still virgins."

I quickly responded, "If that's the case, then my future husband will be among that two percent. No way will I lower my standards and settle for anything less. God will do the finding and choosing for me, and He will give me the best one there is."

I was so sure that God knew best, and I trusted Him concerning that. As I was faithful in praying for my future husband, God revealed to me some verses to give to my future husband when the time came. They gave me an indication of what my calling was to be with my husband:

> But Ruth replied, "Don't ask me to leave you and turn back. Wherever you go, I will go; wherever you live, I will live. Your people will be my people, and your God will be my God. Wherever you die, I will die, and there I will be buried. May the Lord punish me severely if I allow anything but death to separate us!" (Ruth 1:16-17 NLT).

As I prayed over these Scriptures, the Lord showed me that one day I was going to marry someone of a different race from my own ("your people shall be my people") and that I would be traveling and ministering with him in many nations.

VISION FOR FRANCE AND EUROPE

I decided to fast on my 18th birthday and dedicated that day to seeking God for my calling. He visited me in a powerful way and showed me more things concerning my calling, my purpose, and my destiny. In a vision, He showed me revival in France and across Europe. I saw the streets of France filled with crowds of people experiencing revival, healings, and miracles; people were getting saved left and right and the presence and glory of God were filling the place. It was awesome! That was when He gave me a burden to begin praying and interceding for that part of the world. I knew no one who lived there, but God put the French people in my heart and spirit. Although I had no idea how it was going to happen, or what my part would be, I knew that God would order my steps as I chose to follow and obey Him every day.

I remember so well how, during my teenage years, my heart was on fire for God. I was not just in love with Him; I was *passionately* in love with Him. Every waking moment, I was consumed with Him and could only think of ways that I could express my love to Him. I delighted in spending time with Him and serving Him.

When I was 18 and 19, I was in church practically every day. My dad said to me often, "I don't understand you. You practically live at the church. Every day you're there. You come home only to sleep." Since the youth pastors lived in the parsonage right next door to the church, I spent a lot of time there to learn more from them, even when there was nothing going on in church. Sometimes I'd play basketball with them and the youth. To me it was Heaven to be in church or to go to someone's house for Bible study; it was better than being in a negative atmosphere at home with my dad.

There came a point when I felt God telling me to go to the

intercessory prayer time at my church, which was held at six o'clock in the morning. I knew He wanted me to commit to it and not go only when I felt like it. I went faithfully every morning whether it was cold, raining, or snowing, then I went on to school afterward. I loved His presence so much that sometimes I'd fast and pray all day alone in church. I felt like I belonged in God's sanctuary. I delighted myself in His presence as if nothing else mattered. On weekends, instead of going to parties or watching movies, I went street witnessing with some people from church or attended Bible study groups, even at times teaching them. I wanted to tell the whole world about the Love of my life—Jesus! My heart cried this same prayer:

> One thing have I asked of the Lord, that will I seek, inquire for, and [insistently] require: that I may dwell in the house of the Lord [in His presence] all the days of my life, to behold and gaze upon the beauty [the sweet attractiveness and the delightful loveliness] of the Lord and to meditate, consider, and inquire in His temple (Psalm 27:4).

I was so full of God and very satisfied. I was so content with just God and me that marriage was far from my thoughts. I felt no desire for it at all. I didn't feel incomplete because I was not married, nor did I put serving God on hold. I didn't see the need to find a husband in order to serve God. I kept myself busy spending time in His presence. Out of my love for Him, I was seizing every opportunity to make Him known. Eventually, through God's grace, I was able to keep a good attitude at home despite how negative my dad was all the time. Instead of letting it get the best of me, I just kept praising God. At times it was still a struggle, but the Lord always helped me through. Jesus was my defense and my shield and my strength. I just drew closer to Him, and the great thing was, He drew closer to me too.

MIRACLE WITH DAD

One major act of obedience that led to a breakthrough in my relationship with my dad was when God told me to take the initiative in saying to him these three simple words: "I love you." At first I was totally opposed to the idea. I told God that it was my dad's job to say that to me first because he was my father and I was his child. The Lord helped me to realize that my dad couldn't give me what he didn't have. I, on the other hand, had Jesus in my heart, and He could give me the love that I needed, not only for myself, but also more than enough to give to others, especially my dad. I had to learn to love those who hurt me. It was not my own strength or will, but only the power of the Holy Spirit that enabled me to obey. It was the toughest thing I had ever done, but I knew I had to humble myself, obey, and trust Him.

The first time I told my dad that I loved him, he didn't respond at all. So I told God that it didn't work. He said to keep trying and to not give up too easily. And so I persisted. Before long, he started replying, "I love you too." How happy I was the first time I heard those words come out of his mouth! Eventually, my dad started saying it to me first. God is so good! His love is contagious. It can melt even the hardest of hearts. And God gets all the glory each time. Probably the only true love my dad ever received apart from my mom's was the love that God gave me to give to him. And I wanted to let him know that my God is real and loves him too.

Through the suffering I had as a child, I grew closer to the Lord. I now believe that this whole exercise was more for my own good than for any other. I learned obedience, not by following my feelings, but by doing what was right by faith, because God said so in His Word. Consequently, it also removed from my heart any seed of rebellion or resentment toward authority that might otherwise have sprouted and led me into trouble. Forgiving my father didn't mean that what he did was right, but it meant that I put him and all the hurtful things he did and said into God's hands, knowing that God could handle them better than me.

Through my deep and close relationship with God as my Father, I learned to value and honor people in authority and to afford them the same appropriate respect as I did God. It became obvious that, if I did not want to become like my dad and carry over his mistreatment to others and to my future family, I had to break that cycle through love and forgiveness. By allowing God's love to melt and heal all my hurts, I wasn't following my emotions; I was obeying what my spirit knew was right.

Paul describes this action as overcoming evil with good:

Do not repay anyone evil for evil. Be careful to do what is right in the eyes of everybody. If it is possible, as far as it depends on you, live at peace with everyone. Do not take revenge, my friends, but leave room for God's wrath, for it is written: It is mine to avenge; I will repay, says the Lord. On the contrary: If your enemy is hungry, feed him; if he is thirsty, give him something to drink. In doing this, you will heap burning coals on his head. Do not be overcome by evil, but overcome evil with good (Romans 12:17-21 NIV).

God couldn't use me effectively and bless me if I allowed a bitter root to spring forth in my heart (see Heb. 12:15-17). I wouldn't want to walk around with an open wound and minister with an anointing polluted by bitterness. I had to learn to walk in love and forgiveness. I had to learn to love with God's love those who hurt me and spitefully used me. If I succumbed to bitterness, I would be no better than my dad. I thank God that, through His Word and constant guidance, He helped me overcome that area in my life. This was the beginning of my learning to be led by the Spirit rather than by my emotions. That same principle has everything to do with how we end up with God's best.

MOTHER'S LOVE

My mother also helped me a lot. Contrary to my dad's way of showing affection, Mom gave all her children much love, affection, and encouragement. My earliest knowledge and understanding of God came from her. She always referred to the Word of God for every situation. We prayed together a lot, especially when we needed God's intervention at home. I always felt comfortable sharing with her all of my encounters with God and the prophetic dreams that I received. She believed and recognized that God had a special call on my life.

I could open up to my mom without feeling bothered at all

because I knew that she truly loved me and could be trusted. She was always proud of all my achievements. Whenever I had concerts or musicals, and when I graduated, she was there to share those precious moments with me. When it came to dating, she would remind me what the Word of God said about relationships.

chapter 2

DATING—A SET-UP FOR DIVORCE

I knew a young Christian woman who was beautiful, smart, and from a well-to-do family. She and her family were active in their church, and her parents were part of the leadership board. She had started "dating" in the 7th grade. It seemed only natural since her older siblings also dated, and her parents encouraged it as a normal and acceptable part of the teenage culture. It was also then when she had her first kiss. Everyone thought it was so cute!

The teenager subsequently became addicted to dating. She felt the need to continually have a boyfriend; otherwise, she felt lost or feared that she was not cool or beautiful. Entering high school brought dating to a more serious level. However, her serious relationship in high school ended after two years because her parents intervened, feeling that her boyfriend was not good enough for her.

Following the break-up, she found someone else and continued the emotionally destructive cycle of dating throughout college. For four years, despite the fact that she knew he wasn't the one for her, she was involved in a serious relationship with a nice guy who was slightly older. He came from a "good family," but he was not a Christian. She defended the relationship saying that she would rather be with him for the time being than to be alone and unattached.

Finally the young woman "fell in love" with a Christian guy and married him, not because she tested the relationship and knew beforehand that it was of God, but because she was attracted to him physically and emotionally. And, rather than seeking God's input at the beginning, she expected Him to simply bless the relationship after the fact.

Far too many of today's Christian youth and single adults fall into the same trap as this young woman. In fact, most young men and women find their spouses the same way and see absolutely nothing wrong with it. They regard dating as a normal part of life, a necessary step to finding a mate.

When I first entered high school, I too fell into that trap. Fortunately, my dating life never lasted for more than a couple of weeks at a time as I always turned to God and asked Him whether or not it was right. God spared me from a lot of trouble during those few times that I tried dating. Did I find fulfillment in them? No. Although my dating relationships didn't last very long, they were long enough for me to experience physical and emotional attraction. This is "false love," not true love, as betrayal and heartache followed. I learned from those experiences, and they propelled me to seek God for answers and His ways concerning love and relationships.

Deep inside, I knew that God had a better way and that it was totally different from what the world practiced. I began pursuing a way that went against the flow of what everyone else considered normal and good. Consequently, I found myself alone most of the time during this search for truth; but in each step of my journey, the Lord guided me and taught me how I could be the most fulfilled and satisfied in life with just Him—no boyfriend necessary.

It boiled down to getting intimate with Him, letting Him be the One and Only to complete and fulfill me. How? By simply living to know and love Him more each day, to please Him in every way, to be more God-conscious in everything I did, and to consecrate my life to Him and His service. I learned about guarding my heart (will, feelings, and emotions) and keeping it from temptation. *"Keep and guard your heart with all vigilance and above all that you guard, for out of it flow the springs of life"* (Prov. 4:23).

The thing about deception is that you don't know that you're deceived while you're in it. God, in His goodness, lifted the veil from my eyes and allowed me to see the truth for what it was. It was up to me to do something about it. When I finally surrendered my desire for a boyfriend and marriage, focusing my life instead on finding my destiny in God, I was the happiest and the most fulfilled. My greatest joy was spending hours of intimate fellowship in His wonderful presence. Happiness came in doing what pleased God rather than in doing what pleased me.

My desire to please God led naturally to a desire to make right choices along the way. Because I longed to be used by God during this time, my dad's biggest complaint about me was that I was always at church or at Bible studies during the week. It seemed to him as though I practically lived there and came home only to sleep. He couldn't understand my devotion to God or my desire to serve Him.

As I sensed the Lord leading me to write this book, He told me that dating is a detrimental practice for His children and that it is actually a set-up for divorce. Dating is not a preparation for marriage, as most people think it is. At first, I was shocked at this revelation until He showed me that every principle in dating goes against His ways. This is one reason why the Church experiences similar problems and heartaches as the world when it comes to marriage and relationships. Dating was never part of God's plan for us.

Dating—An All-American Innovation

Much of the wisdom in this section is taken from the excellent book, *Choosing God's Best* by Don Raunikar.[1] I highly recommend his book for the insights that he shares about dating.

Dating did not originate with God. Dating in the United States began in the early 1900s. Until that time, almost everything involving young people's activities revolved around the home and family. Instead of dating, there was *courtship,* a carefully controlled "calling" system governed by rules covering conversation, chaperonage, and length of visits—each a test of suitability, breeding, and background.

As the United States became more urban and industrial, "calling" became less practical as families lived in only one or two rooms. Keeping company in the family parlor was replaced with couples going dining, dancing, and to the movies. Courtship went public and became "dating." Also at this time—1910-1945—young women began taking advantage of new opportunities such as attending college, working outside the home, and entering urban professions. In addition, widespread use of the automobile gave couples more mobility and privacy, leading to what was called "parking."[2]

The new dating system gave young men and women more freedom. Courtship had taken place in the girl's home or at functions largely devised by and presided over by women. Dating moved courtship out of the home and into the man's sphere—outside the home. This took away an element of protection for the woman. Dating became more about competition and popularity.

After World War II, women outnumbered men for the first time in U.S. history. By 1950, "going steady" meant a guaranteed date and greater sexual intimacy. Just as this rating/dating system was making an exit, America experienced its highest ever marriage rate while at the same time the average age at marriage fell dramatically. Because girls were marrying at 18 and boys at 20, the preparation for marriage ("shopping around") had to begin in the mid-teens.[3]

According to Dr. Raunikar:

> Misguided sociologists told parents to help their
> children become datable by putting them in situations
> that would allow them to begin dating. The strategy

was that, ideally, each boy and girl should date and know 25-50 eligible marriage partners before making a final decision.

This new dating philosophy meant many more partners, all of whom were potential partners for necking, petting, and sexual involvement. It promoted sexual experimentation not only through the privacy it offered but also through the sense of obligation it fostered: The man paid for everything and the woman became indebted. The more money the man spent, the more physical involvement he felt he was owed.

A significant percentage of youth had premarital intercourse during and before the "going steady" years, but sex before marriage did not become conventional behavior until the mid-1960s. By then, the nation was moving toward a sexual revolution that would create moral dilemmas unparalleled in U.S. history.

Before the "Make Love, Not War" philosophies of the Vietnam War era, society expected individuals not to be sexually involved before marriage. Today, as most singles will attest, sexual involvement is an unwritten expectation on the first date. By age nineteen, 86 percent of unmarried males are having sexual intercourse.[4]

Not only have we exported "dating" around the world (via television and movies) as the means to finding love and romance, we are also seeing the resulting downward spiral of society and the destructive results in relationships and marriages that end in divorce, not to mention the increase in abortion, sexually transmitted diseases, illegitimate births, premature marriages, single parenting, etc.

Today love and romance (sex and short-term affairs) are enjoyed solely for recreational value. Movies and television regularly show relationships with no long-term commitment. Television programs promote dating situations in which someone dates several different girls or guys and then picks the one they like the best and possibly marries the winner. I wonder how many of those relationships are actually successful in the long run.

What are the values of dating that everybody needs to know and understand? How does it oppose God's way of uniting two people? As I saw the great need in our society to know God's truth about this matter, the Lord put heavily in my heart to research and study the subject as well as to pray and fast in order to bring the truth to light. *"And you will know the truth, and the truth will set you free"* (John 8:32 NLT). In order to know the truth, one must seek it out and value it like a hidden treasure until it is found. Once you find it, to truly know what it means, you must learn and apply it as an essential part of your life. But *unless you know the truth concerning dating and its negative results, you'll approve of it, fall into its trap, and suffer its consequences.* When something is in darkness, it cannot be dispelled until it is brought into the light. Healing, breakthrough, and change cannot begin until the sin is revealed. Please have an open heart and mind concerning this truth about dating. May the Lord set you free.

DATING PRINCIPLES

Contrary to popular perception, I believe that dating is a set-up for divorce due to the fact that the principles and practices of dating encourage attitudes and behaviors that are contrary to God's standards for healthy relationships. How is this so? What are the basic principles of dating? How is dating opposed to God's way of uniting couples? Consider the following:

- Dating is flesh-centered (satisfies fleshly desires) rather than God-centered (submitted to what God desires for us).

- Dating is self-centered. It feeds on the selfish human tendency to value other people for the personal needs they can fill and the personal happiness they can provide (the "what have you done for me lately?" mindset).

- The goal of dating is to satisfy a short-term physical and/or emotional need, not a lifelong commitment. Dating holds in highest regard physical, romantic attraction and intimacy, but it avoids commitment and responsibility.

- While dating, a couple may have marriage in mind as the ultimate goal, but the focus is on the short-term goal of immediate pleasure with no care for the consequences.

- Dating places little emphasis on how to develop healthy relationships, how to choose the right mate, or how to prepare for marriage. It focuses instead on short-term physical and emotional satisfaction that requires little or no commitment.

- Dating promotes the idea that, because people can get over past relationships, the best approach is to "shop around" and "try on" different people to see which one suits the best—exchanging partners freely for ones who "fit better."

- Dating underestimates the power of one person in another person's life. Marriage does not erase the emotional scars and guilt of past sins and past relationships. Those scars can haunt and hurt a marriage for a lifetime.

- Dating often mistakes physical attraction for love.

- Dating distorts the real by obscuring distinctions and absolutes. There are no standards, no right and wrong, and no boundaries. The only thing that matters is what feels good at the moment. Dating promotes sexual indulgence and leads easily to premarital sex.

- The dating motto is "see and conquer!"

- Dating doesn't value friendship as the beginning and most important part of a relationship.

- Dating creates a superficial environment for evaluating another person's character and life.

- Dating often isolates a couple from other important relationships such as family and friends. They become obsessive about being together and spend most of their time alone in isolated locations.

These dating principles are contrary to God's plan of wholeness and fulfillment.

WORLDWIDE DECEPTION

During one of our annual trips to Israel, my husband, David, took our daughter and me to lunch at a nearby hotel. The manager, an Israeli woman, kept staring at us as she lunched with two young girls. Finally she spoke to us and said that she couldn't help but look at us because she thought we were a beautiful family. I asked if the two girls were her daughters. She said that one of them was but that the other one was her 12-year-old son's girlfriend who was staying with them. Remarking how today's children start dating at a young age, she admitted that she simply accepted it and let them "go steady."

I politely disagreed. She felt there was nothing she could do because children today want what they want. Children want to copy what they see on television and in the movies. When we left the restaurant, my heart sank as I realized how we are losing this generation to sin and godlessness. Something radical has to take place to save it.

In America and worldwide, the same is true; children even younger than 12 are dating and experimenting with sex. What they call freedom—free to do whatever pleases them—is really bondage because they are bound and oppressed by a sinful lifestyle. God tells parents: *"Point your kids in the right direction—when they're old they won't be lost*" (Prov. 22:6 TM). "*He who spares his rod [of discipline] hates his son, but he who loves him disciplines diligently and punishes him early*" (Prov. 13:24). Neither of these verses tell parents to give their children whatever they want; there must be boundaries and direction.

Dating eventually results in inherent problems, including "falling in lust" rather than falling in love. I've heard people say, "*Date so you can find a mate before it's too late.*" Some may seriously date the same person for a very long time without the relationship ever ending in marriage. Imagine the intensity of the heartache when they part. Those who date often and with many different people are not only damaging their own sense of self-worth, but they also run the fatal risk of contracting a sexual disease. The key element in dating seems to be self-indulgence, which is totally opposed to God's ways.

Another detrimental element of dating is that it often eliminates the friendship phase that is so vital to all healthy relationships. One-on-one dating most times propels a man and woman beyond friendship in a rush toward romance and physical involvement. When physical and emotional involvement becomes the focus, there is no time to develop true friendship. Friendship removes the pressure to perform in a relationship because friends feel free to relax and be themselves without the need either to look perfect or to impress each other. Friends enjoy each other's company for its own sake, with no hidden agendas and no rush or even desire to become romantically involved.

For many people, dating is a way to enjoy the emotional and physical benefits of intimacy without the responsibility of a true commitment. The fallacy with this idea is that true intimacy is impossible without commitment. True intimacy is more than just the close proximity of bodies; it also involves the joining of heart, mind, and spirit with the other person.

An intimate relationship is a beautiful experience that God created for us to enjoy (see Gen. 1:27-28; 2:18-25), but only in the context of a commitment-based love within the parameters of marriage. A relationship based only on physical attraction and romantic feelings will last only as long as the feelings last. But even if the relationship has marriage as the direction of their commitment, heavy petting, "making out," oral sex, and actual sex are still damaging. Once the feelings are gone, so is the commitment (and the relationship), leaving broken hearts and wounded spirits.

THE SUPERFICIAL ENVIRONMENT OF DATING

Romantic attraction is the main frame of dating, but this can be very deceptive. *Dating creates a superficial environment that doesn't demand either party to honestly portray their positive and negative characteristics.* Are they really getting to know each other for who they really are in this kind of relationship or setting? Or are they both just putting up a likable face and personality, doing whatever the other person likes or expects? After their relationship is over, many go back to their old self because there's no longer anyone to impress or perform for. Few people are ever truly themselves on a date. How can something real and beautiful come out of such superficiality and deception?

People can charm their way into the other's hearts. Being fun to be with on a date doesn't say anything about a person's true character or ability to be a good, dependable, and godly husband or wife. Two people contemplating marriage need to make sure that they are not basing their decision simply on the fun and romantic settings of dating. Going out on a date actually means taking a break from the reality and pressures of life. It may be fun and romantic, but it is not real life. Couples pondering marriage need a strong measure of objective reality. They need to see each other in real-life settings. They need to observe how each other acts around family, friends, and church leaders who know them well, and need to see how they each deal with the normal stresses and pressures of everyday life.

When considering a potential mate, it is important to know who he or she really is. What about her relationship with her father, mother, siblings, spiritual leaders, boss, friends, and enemies? How about the way he reacts to children, opposition, stress, criticism, correction, not getting his way, etc. After couples spend some time together, do they tend to want to reprogram the other person into someone different? Often those changes, if they're at all applied, will only be temporary efforts at pleasing and winning the other's heart. People will eventually revert to how they really.

ENDNOTES

1. Donald F. Raunikar, *Choosing God's Best* (Colorado Springs, CO: Multnomah Publishing Group, 1998), 34-38.

2. Ibid., 36.

3. Ibid., 36.

4. Ibid., 37-38.

The Truth About Dating

There are many reasons why I believe that God should be your matchmaker—many are based on the truth about dating. The following information about dating sheds light on how devastating dating can be—especially if you don't understand its ultimate consequences.

Characteristics of Dating

How can dating be responsible for broken hearts and marriages? Here are several explanations:

- Dating typically begins in the early teen years when there is no concern for marriage, yet physical and emotional bonding are permitted and treated casually.

- Dating teens often receive little guidance, protection, and involvement from parents or spiritual leaders. Complete privacy in dating is permitted, expected, and encouraged. Relationships outside the home and family are formed.

- Dating does not teach people how to relate to the opposite sex. On the contrary, it sows seeds of regret through inappropriate involvement with the opposite sex. It damages, rather than develops, social and emotional health.

- Dating gives too much freedom to young people, more than most of them can handle appropriately without teaching, preparation, or guidance in handling their relationships and their hormones. Often their only model is the twisted example of Hollywood. Dating provides no true boundaries or rules to respect. There is little or no accountability.

- Dating couples pair up mainly on the basis of fun, romance, and physical attraction, typically mistaking lust and infatuation for love.

- Dating can quickly replace fun with pain and romance with hurt and resentment.

- Dating encourages "safe sex" instead of abstinence.

DIFFERENT TYPES OF DATING RELATIONSHIPS

Since dating is more flesh-centered than it is God-centered (people choosing their mates instead of God), Christians reap more devastating results than non-Christians because they know better what is right and wrong, what is godly and what is fleshly. So in a way, Christians are more accountable to God and more conscious of what they are doing. Dating is a worldly practice, even though many call it "Christian dating," and attaching a Christian label to it does not make it a right or God-approved practice, regardless of how well it is accepted by the Church. The following are some forms of dating that many Christians practice, which are flesh-centered and have dire consequences:

Missionary Dating

This is when a Christian dates a non-Christian in an attempt to win that person to the Lord. This is one of the biggest deceptions ever! This type of relationship is clearly spoken about in the Bible—as something *not* to do. Intellectually people know that a conversion is unlikely, but they convince themselves that somehow God didn't really mean it that way or that their relationship is an exception and that God understands their heart.

But the Word is crystal clear:

Don't become partners with those who reject God. How can you make a partnership out of right and wrong? That's not partnership; that's war. Is light best friends with dark? Does Christ go strolling with the Devil? Do trust and mistrust hold hands? Who would think of setting up pagan idols in God's holy Temple? But that is exactly what we are, each of us a temple in whom God lives. God Himself put it this way: I'll live in them, move into them; I'll be their God and they'll be My people. So leave the corruption and compromise; leave it for good, says God. Don't link up with those who will pollute you. I want you all for Myself. I'll be a Father to you; you'll be sons and daughters to Me. The Word of the Master, God (2 Corinthians 6:14-18 TM).

When someone marries a person who does not share their love and desire for God, that person may divide, control, or even prohibit them from their commitment to God. I knew a Christian girl who dated a non-Christian from her homeland. They had a long-distance relationship. She took trips to spend time with him, and after one such trip, she told me she was engaged. I asked her if he was saved. She said that he wasn't but that he had agreed to go to church when he came to America a week before their wedding. So he came, went to church, and even prayed the sinner's prayer. She was so happy, but I still didn't have a peace about him. I knew that she was going about this whole thing the wrong way, but she had already set her heart to go all the way with it. Even the church approved of their relationship, so shortly they were married.

A couple of weeks later, I received a phone call from the young woman saying sadly that she couldn't attend church because her husband wouldn't allow it. She was miserable and in deep regret. The romance before the wedding had faded quickly. He only prayed the sinner's prayer to please her just so that he could marry her. The real person finally came out, and he wasn't at all the person she thought she knew. He had no intentions of living for God, much less allow her to attend church. What a rude awakening! She lost more than what she was prepared to surrender.

God would not force her to marry His choice, but neither would He prevent her from marrying her choice. The enemy of God's best is not settling for something or someone bad, but what is good, or good enough. *Not every good choice is God's choice,* and the difference can radically affect the rest of your life.

A non-Christian may show interest in God only to gain an advantage over a believer. A believer may want desperately to believe the interest is genuine and may think that he or she is "in love." Because most who find themselves in this situation have already let their fleshly desires take over, they justify being in this ungodly relationship and ignore God's Word. They allow themselves to be lost in a sea of deception. They've already bought into the lie of the enemy that the relationship will bring them the happiness and fulfillment they long for. But to "fall in love" with someone, whether Christian or not, does not equate being in the will of God, especially when God is not even involved in it.

Believers must come to grips with the strong possibility that their unsaved love interest will not get saved. What would they do then? Where would their loyalty be then? Will they give up God just to be with that person? There's no need to pray and ask God if it's His will to be with an unbeliever when God already said in His Word where He stands concerning an unequal yoke or union. When people marry anyway, the consequences are far more detrimental, not only as a couple, but more so to their children. Remember, just because a person prays the sinner's prayer doesn't mean there is a true conversion to Christ. Genuine change and a desire to be discipled and delivered from bondage need to be evident.

People should not be fooled or forced to settle for someone they have to "fix" in order to conform to their standards. God has a much better match—a perfect match, someone who shares their standards and whose character and personality will complement theirs—if they will only trust Him to bring that person into their lives in His timing. If they want the best choice, leave the choosing, arranging, and timing to God alone. Settle only for God's best, not for someone good enough or second best.

Hero Dating

Another unhealthy dating environment is hero dating. Under this category, there are two scenarios. The first one is when one person is much stronger spiritually than the other. The spiritually stronger person dates those who need "saving"—they need to rescue their date from a crisis or fix their problem for them. They are happy only when they are saving someone they believe is in trouble.

Today's terminology for this type of relationship is "codependent." Codependent people never say "no" to those who ask for help. Many times they volunteer to help people who are immature and irresponsible. But as they constantly step in and rescue the person from the natural consequences of their bad choices, it takes a toll on them not just physically, but also emotionally, mentally, financially, materially, and spiritually. All the while, the ones they are saving continue in their destructive and irresponsible ways because they never learn the hard lessons.

These heroes don't realize that, first, they are taking the place of Jesus as that person's Savior. Instead of relying on Jesus, the needy ones rely on their heroes. Second, they are teaching others not to take responsibility for their own mistakes or wrong decisions. Third, they are encouraging others to remain immature and to not learn how to solve their problems. Self-appointed heroes cannot meet every need that another person has. Yes, God may use them to help others, but by stepping in each time, they are also robbing someone else of their blessing. Sometimes the answer is something that these needy people can come up with themselves, but they will never realize that, develop critical thinking skills, or gain their independence if their heroes keep rescuing them. This is not a godly or healthy relationship.

The second scenario in hero dating is when the stronger person tries hard to bring the weaker one into greater spiritual maturity, usually with limited success. A dating relationship—and even more so a marriage—is not the place for one partner to seek to develop the other's character and spiritual growth. If godly character is not present or in progress at the beginning of the relationship, there is no guarantee that it will develop later.

Some people will make superficial changes in order to win their partner's heart and approval, only to revert back to their old ways and habits. More often than not, the weaker ones carry many hurts and unresolved issues that cause a lot of marital trouble. I have known many couples who suffered tremendously in their marriages due to this, with some ending in divorce.

Reckless Dating

When people get desperate, they take drastic measures to make things happen. They make up many reasons to justify their needs, longings, and actions. Some say that they can't control their lusts and think marriage will solve the problem. But that same lust can be brought into the marriage when it is not dealt with, and it can cause a lot of hurt through adulterous affairs, sexual abuse, pornography, and rape. *Marriage is not the solution for lust.* The only cure is to receive deliverance from it as a single.

Sometimes the ticking of their biological clock makes people realize that they are not getting any younger. They get impatient—a sign that they are not trusting God for their future and not letting Him be the only source of wholeness and happiness. They are deceived into thinking that a human being can meet all their needs and that God can't. They have false expectations about marriage. They take matters into their own hands. That's how Ishmael was conceived—making something happen in the flesh, and not in the Spirit (see Gen. 16). Solving problems in the flesh always ends in defeat, regret, shame, and misery. But we will always win and be totally blessed when we let God do it.

Some people allow loneliness to bring such agonizing pain into their hearts that they want to jump into someone's arms (or someone's bed) for love and comfort, thinking it will solve their loneliness. Some single parents get so weighed down by the stress of parenting alone that they succumb to the flesh to alleviate the pressure. They are desperate to have someone love them and share the burden of parenting, but they don't realize that *dating is not the cure for loneliness.*

First of all, they are looking for love and fulfillment outside of God and His will. Instead of approaching God with an attitude of, *What can I do for You and Your Kingdom? How can I use my singleness for Your glory? How can I serve and be a blessing to others?,* they allow worldliness to influence their hearts and minds and derail their focus from God.

Instead, they approach God and say, *What have You done for me lately?* It's all about me, me, me! Singles who date out of desperation devalue themselves. Many even accept unconscionable behavior and treatment from their lover that they greatly regret later.

Internet Dating

Millions are relying on Internet dating services, rather than God, to choose their mates. Dating services match people with eligible candidates to see which one suits them best. Their decisions are based strictly on physical attraction and answers to a one-size-fits-all questionnaire. In reality, though, there are things that they don't know about themselves or the other person that only God knows, which makes Him the only One eligible to be *The* Matchmaker. These services are not fool proof, and there are many opportunities for deception and falsehood. Using the latest technology to match people pits humans against God, deceiving us into believing that we have what it takes to make a perfect match.

Some people connect with total strangers via chat rooms on the Internet. Many risk getting engaged before even meeting the person. Some even marry people they have known only through typing messages to them over the Internet. I've heard about couples who have traveled across a continent to meet someone for the very first time and get married. I'm talking about *Christians* and *churches* that condone and marry couples from this kind of relationship.

Once after he returned from preaching in Kuwait, David told me about two Christian Indian girls in their early 20s who were contemplating meeting two older Christian businessmen in person that they had been chatting with through the Internet. They asked David his opinion about meeting them with the purpose of marrying them. David strongly advised them not to, explaining why it is dangerous and biblically wrong, and told them about the right way to find a mate. I believe they listened to him and heeded his warnings.

I have known people who willfully rejected every godly warning and counsel concerning this type of arrangement and ended up living with life-threatening abuse and eventually divorcing. Many singles from third world countries, out of desperation to get out of their misery, marry the first American they meet through the Internet—whether through chat rooms or a dating service. On the other hand, I have heard that there are also many American men, mostly older and divorced, who look for young exotic women from third world countries to marry for companionship or to pleasure them via the Internet. They deceive themselves into thinking that they are saving these poor women from misery. They justify their actions as being compassionate and heroic; in reality they simply want someone to satisfy their fleshly desires and lusts.

We cannot say a match made in this way is from God, is ordained by God, or is a gift from God. There's nothing divine or supernatural about it. The world invented it because they don't acknowledge or rely on God for their relationships; but now Christians are adapting this secular way of finding a mate too. The only way a relationship can be considered from God is if the whole thing (the who, the when, and the how) is all God. How can people know that they are ready for marriage, or if marriage is even God's will for them at that time of their life? Just because they want a mate doesn't mean they should get one. *Beware of labeling something that's manmade and calling it God.*

Queenly Treatment Dating

Many men will bend over backward to impress the woman they want—treating her as a queen. In many cases, these are women who have low self-esteem, are insecure, and are desperate for a man's love and attention. They easily fall into the queenly trap. After they marry the man who gave them such queenly treatment, the treatment stops. Most of the time, these women find themselves in a servant role and are expected to treat the man like a king, which they usually do out of a sense of indebtedness—and out of fear that if they don't, they will find themselves alone again. It should come as no surprise then, that women who fall for the queenly treatment trap often end up in abusive relationships from which they feel there is no escape.

DANGEROUS CONSEQUENCES

In much of Western society, children who are 12 years of age or even younger already have boyfriends and girlfriends, and some are experimenting with sex. Adolescents should not date—it isn't a safe or healthy environment for them to be alone with the opposite sex. Every two minutes in the United States, someone is sexually assaulted. In 2006, there were more than 272,300 victims of rape, attempted rape, or sexual assault.[1]

Another danger of dating is that boys and girls come with different expectations. Most girls seek to feel loved, wanted, and secure. Most boys, on the other hand, usually have one thing in mind—sex. This places enormous pressure on the girl who thinks that she has to give the guy what he wants. Different needs and different expectations equal trouble. Conversely, God will meet all of our needs without causing trouble that will haunt us for life.

Parents who allow their children to date remove them from the security, guidance, and protection that they very much still need. Giving children too much independence prematurely is a sure-fire ticket to hurt and heartache. Just because teenagers' bodies resemble those of adults does not mean they are ready for sex. Teenagers are not mentally, emotionally, or financially ready to deal maturely with the consequences and responsibilities of caring for a baby, forming a family, or facing a life tainted with sexually transmitted diseases. Wholesome friendship is what they truly need, for in that context they can develop healthy relationship skills without compromising either their sexuality or their innocence and without giving up vital parental involvement in their lives. Friendship shields young people from the emotional pain of breaking up that is an inevitable part of the dating game.

People date primarily to cure their loneliness. Some just want to have fun and enjoy the companionship of others or to find a little romance. Their intentions may sound sincere and genuine, but we must not overlook the negative and dangerous results. *Do not sell yourself short for something that will give you only temporary satisfaction and leave you with permanent damage.*

The media loves to display the fun and romantic side of dating and sex, mostly outside the context of marriage. They make it appear fascinating and wonderful, purposely concealing all of the negative, damaging, and hurtful consequences. As a result, AIDS and other sexually transmitted diseases are rampant worldwide. The media more often than not neglects to show the results of a life thrown into turmoil when a young girl becomes pregnant and thinks that she must either abort the child, move in with a guy she hardly knows, or get married because of the pregnancy. Movies and television shows don't show the girl crying herself to sleep night after night.

Most people underestimate and overlook the permanent damage, curses, and transference of unclean spirits that result from sexual involvement outside of a marriage arranged by God. Dating is one of the byproducts of a generally more permissive and promiscuous culture that can produce countless damaging effects in the marriages that follow. These consequences may include (but are not limited to):

- Sexually-transmitted diseases (STDs), especially among youth. The Center for Disease Control estimates that approximately 19 million new infections occur each year, almost half of them among young people ages 15 to 24.[2]

- Divorce. According to the Barna Research Group:

   While it may be alarming to discover *that born-again*

Christians are more likely than others to experience a divorce, that pattern has been in place for quite some time.... But the research also raises questions regarding the effectiveness of how churches minister to families. The ultimate responsibility for a marriage belongs to the husband and wife, but the high incidence of divorce within the Christian community challenges the idea that churches truly provide practical and life-changing support for marriages (emphasis added).

George Barna also said that the results cause "questions regarding the effectiveness of how churches minister to families." He added, "We rarely find substantial differences between the moral behavior of Christians and non-Christians."[3]

Donald Hughes, author of *The Divorce Reality*, said: "In the churches, people have a superstitious view that Christianity will keep them from divorce, but they are subject to the same problems as everyone else, and *they include a lack of relationship skills. Just being born again is not a rabbit's foot*" (emphasis added). Hughes claims that 90 percent of born again couples who divorce do so *after* they have been saved.[4]

There is something more to being a Christian. Just saying that you are a born-again Christian does not guarantee that you will have a successful marriage or that your marriage will be a powerful witness to non-believers that glorifies God. It takes a lot of hard work, dying to self, unconditional love, humility, and commitment from both husband and wife for a marriage to grow, improve, and work. You must do away with pride, stubbornness, bad attitudes and habits. You should value each other and your marriage enough to seek help when you need it and to look for ways to constantly improve it, making it what God designed it to be. Your marriage should reflect the love and intimacy that God has with His Bride—the Church.

Other damaging consequences include:

- Date rape, sexual addiction, and promiscuity.

- An increase in teen and unwanted pregnancies and in illegitimate children. Who suffers the consequences of early sexual activity? Teenage mothers are less likely to complete high school (only one third receive a high school diploma), and only 1.5 percent earn a college degree by age 30. Nearly 80 percent of unmarried teen mothers are more likely to end up on welfare. The children of teenage mothers have lower birth weights, are more likely to perform poorly in school, and are at greater risk for abuse and neglect. Sons of teen mothers are 13 percent more likely to end up in prison while teen daughters are 22 percent more likely to become teen mothers themselves.[5]

- Millions of unborn babies are aborted. More than 40 million abortions have been performed in the United States since 1973.[6]

- The heartache of breaking up. It is devastating when you give yourself to someone emotionally and physically and then that someone decides that you are not the right person and moves on to another. The cycle never stops; neither do the debilitating results.

It's never easy to do what is right, but *as God's child, you are not to choose what is easy over what is right.* Your allegiance is to God and not to yourself or anyone else. By breaking off the relationship without delay, even though it is difficult to do, you are positioning yourself on God's side, the winning side. Then as you surrender everything to Him, you can be restored to wholeness by breaking off all counterfeit ties with your past loves or lovers (more about this in Chapter 5), and by becoming intimate with Jesus you will discover Him to be the source of satisfaction, fulfillment, and wholeness.

Because of the wounds from break-ups, there are a lot of hurting people in our society. It is hard for them to know how to form healthy, wholesome relationships, especially because they continue the destructive cycle of dating. *Wounded people tend to wound people.* There are dire consequences when a hurt person marries another hurt person. That combination is a recipe for disaster. The cycle of hurt continues even after they have their own family because marriage will not heal the hurts. It is better that hurting people remain single and use that time to deal with issues and hurts, becoming healed and whole in Jesus.

Often married people who dated experience a myriad of negative outcomes with their mates, like a tendency to be easily angered, to easily take offence, to be abusive, or to be incapable of giving encouragement, compliments, trust, forgiveness, satisfying sex, and so on. The pain from the past can linger and infect the present. Satan wants the woman who was hurt to spend the remainder of her life hating the man who hurt her—and better yet, he wants the bitterness to evolve into a hatred toward all men. The same is true of wounded men.

God's plan is for us to forgive those who hurt us. It doesn't mean that what they did was OK, but forgiveness is the only way that we can be healed, set free, and forgiven of our own sins. It's not enough to have Jesus in our hearts. *We must commit to following God's plan and ways so that healing and wholeness can take place in our hearts.* Sometimes pain pushes some people toward obedience. When the pain of dating is greater than the payback, then people are ready for a change, an alternative.

I believe that one of the most common causes for marital problems among couples is their involvement in the dating system before marriage. Pain, resentment, disillusionment, and other negative experiences from failed relationships transfer into their marriage as emotional baggage that weighs down the relationship and creates formidable obstacles for the couple to overcome—ultimately inhibiting the development of true intimacy. Even their children feel the effects as some face multiple family break-ups during childhood.

LOVE AND OBEDIENCE

Following God's ways spares us a lot of heartache. We need to learn to listen and obey God the first time that He speaks to us. Learning from obedience is better than learning from disobedience (see 1 Sam. 15:22). Love and obedience go hand-in-hand. Obedience is proof of our love. If we say we love God yet disobey Him, then we don't truly love Him (see 1 John 5:3). Then we are not acting as true children of God, but as illegitimate children (see Heb. 12:8). Surely God's grace is broad and expansive. Though many may think, *Our love and obedience toward Him will never be perfect in this life,* this is no excuse for sinning and thinking, *Oh well, nobody's perfect.* But as committed disciples of Christ, we should always be perfecting and maturing in our love for Him (see Phil. 3:12).

I teach this principle to my children: if you obey your parents quickly the first time that you are asked to do something, then when God asks you to do something, you will be quick to obey Him the first time too. This way they won't need a hundred confirmations before deciding to do what God says. The earlier children learn how to hear and obey God's voice, the earlier they will learn to trust Him at a deep level and discover how He rewards those who truly love Him through their lifestyle of obedience.

Of course, dating is not solely responsible for these sobering realities. But there's no doubt that our permissive dating culture contributes to a majority of today's societal troubles. Is dating worth the resulting trouble? Is there a better way? Yes, there is a better way; but first the Church must wake up, acknowledging its role in contributing to the problem and taking steps to turn things around.

ENDNOTES

1. "How often does sexual assault occur?" *Rape, Abuse and Incest National Network*, http://www.rainn.org/get-information /statistics/frequency-of-sexual-assault (accessed 10 September 2008).

2. "STD Surveillance 2006," *Centers for Disease Control and Prevention*, http://www.cdc.gov/std/stats/trends2006 .htm (accessed 10 September 2008).

3. "Christians are more likely to experience divorce than are non-Christians," *The Barna Group*, quoted in B.A. Robinson, "U.S. divorce rates for various faith groups, age groups and geographic areas," *Ontario Consultants on Religious Tolerance*, http://www.religioustoleance.org/chr_dira .htm (accessed 11 September 2008).

4. Donald Hughes, *The Divorce Reality*, quoted in *Ibid*.

5. "The DCR Report," *The National Campaign to Prevent Teen and Unplanned Pregnancy*, http://www.thenational campaign.org/resources/dcr/ (accessed 11 September 2008).

6. "Over 40 Million Abortions in U.S. since 1973," *National Right to Life*, http://www.nrlc.org/ABORTION/ABO RAMT.HTML (accessed 11 September 2008).

chapter 4

DATING AND THE CHURCH

David and I knew a 17-year-old Christian girl who was dating a 22-year-old man from her church. Their parents accepted their relationship and laid down rules and limits. Her mother told her daughter that she was not to show any more affection to her boyfriend that she would show to her own father. The young woman agreed.

During the time that David and I were guests in their home, while ministering in their area, we noticed that the young woman was totally comfortable showing much affection to her boyfriend. Although she had told her parents that he wasn't the "right one," and they had agreed that there was no future to their relationship, they still allowed her to date him. David and I couldn't help but think that the couple was wasting their time *and* emotions just for the sake of being in a relationship.

How many other Christian singles are like this couple? How many Christian parents today take the same permissive attitude toward their children's relationships? God says, *"Don't copy the behavior and customs of this world, but let God transform you into a new person by changing the way you think. Then you will learn to know God's will for you, which is good and pleasing and perfect"* (Rom. 12:2 NLT).

In this very critical area of life—as in many others—many have disobeyed the Lord's clear instructions to *not* copy the behavior and customs of this world. Somehow it seems that most of the Church interprets Romans 12:2 quite differently from what it plainly says. We may hear it preached, but generally we poorly enforced it in our daily lives. Most have not changed their ways by the renewing of their minds—by the cultivation of a completely different and distinct mindset from that of the world. We need to simply learn and apply *His* ways in order to have *His* mindset. That's the only way that we'll know for certain what is God's good, pleasing, and perfect will for us.

Having grown up in Church, and now as a minister who travels worldwide, I have seen how most of the Church has embraced the culture of dating. I've seen the full spectrum of extremities— extreme grace as well as extreme legalism. Growing up, I heard holiness preached a lot, especially at youth camps. Regrettably, the call to holiness was rarely enforced or followed up on. There was no discipline or consequences, even for obvious sin issues. Dating was an acceptable norm. Flirting, public displays of affection (PDA), and teasing were also tolerated. Very few went against the flow.

To make things worse, I was deeply disappointed to learn that some of the very people who preached strongly on holiness at our youth camp later fell into sin with their secretaries. At another church, the pastor's teenage daughter got pregnant and tried to hide it from the church. Something is terribly wrong with this picture. These types of issues need to be addressed if we want to see a positive change in the Body of Christ. *Believers have to value, seek out, and practice true holiness from God, without legalism yet without compromise.*

CHRISTIAN DATING

See to it that no one takes you captive through hollow and deceptive philosophy, which depends on human tradition and the basic principles of this world rather than on Christ (Colossians 2:8 NIV).

Dating did not originate in the Bible or even in the Church but in secular society. The Church, by and large, however, has bought into the practice, thus "Christianizing" it. This can be a subtle but deadly trap. The Scripture in Colossians indicates that, as believers, we must beware of deceptive philosophies and traditions of man that can pull us away from God's ways. "Christian" dating is essentially a contradiction in terms because there is nothing Christian about it. Yet in my experience, many Christians and Church leaders endorse the practice with apparently no sense of contradiction or conviction. I have found that these are some of the most common characteristics and principles that comprise much of "Christian" dating:

- Though labeled Christian, dating is still mainly flesh-centered instead of God-centered. Rather than God, often Hollywood is the main influence in behavior and relationships, which sends out a confusing message to the world.

- Couples pair up mainly on the basis of romantic and physical attraction and fun. There is little or no vision as to why two people should be put together with regard to God's purposes. God's will is not given priority.

- Christians date to satisfy a short-term physical or emotional need, not a lifelong commitment. Thus, they hold the physical and emotional attraction in highest esteem, mistaking infatuation for love and avoiding commitment and responsibility.

- Many dating Christian couples assume that anything physical is permissible as long as they avoid the actual sex act; but far too many reach that point and find themselves unable to stop. Some do not even set that limit, as some parents encourage safe sex instead of abstinence.

- Many dates that result in physical intimacy do not lead to commitment and marriage.

- Just like unbelievers, many Christian youth typically begin dating in their early teens, and physical and emotional bonding are treated casually.

- Too much freedom is given to young people, which leads to inappropriate behavior. They are free to choose who they date, where they go, and what they do. Curfew is often the only restriction that parents enforce. Relationships outside the home and family are formed.

- Young people receive little or no guidance, protection, preparation, accountability, or involvement from parents or spiritual leaders. Many youth are not educated by parents or spiritual leaders about preparing for a godly marriage and waiting and trusting in God for their mate. Adult involvement usually consists of being introduced to whoever their kids are already dating and arranging wedding plans.

- Dating is encouraged more than the development of healthy friendships with the opposite sex. Many churches do not teach or provide information to their youth and single adults about how to relate to the opposite sex in a wholesome way, without getting romantically involved. Thus they do more damage rather than helping their singles develop social and emotional health. Some parents are happy and even relieved to see their children date. They see it as evidence that their children are socially acceptable.

- The idea is promoted that past relationships, good and bad, are easy to get over, so youth are encouraged to "shop around" until the "right" person is found. Young people are not warned that their fun can be quickly replaced with hurt, and their romance with heartache, as each casual relationship ends. Many assume that marriage will erase the emotional scars and guilt from their past relationships, unaware that, in reality, those issues may affect and hurt their marriages.

- The reality: the type, quality, conduct, and commitment level of "Christian" dates are usually not much different from those of non-Christians.

Notice the similarities between this list and the worldly dating and its principles list in the previous chapter? Christian singles across America and around the world have embraced dating and found themselves in destructive relationships that affect their lives forever. How can we as serious Christians—as a people set apart for God—embrace such a practice when its very principles go completely against God's? The Bible does not teach casual dating, where we can "try on" different people or "shop around" until we find one who fits. Neither does it teach entering into romantic relationships without marriage as a goal. *Just because it's the social norm doesn't mean that it should be the Christian norm.*

WRONG PAIRS

I knew a girl who was fired up for God. She had a burning desire to go to other countries and minister to orphans and abused children. Then she met someone who had a burden for America. They ended up dating each other, getting married, having children, and pastoring in the United States. I believe they had two different visions and callings, but she sacrificed her vision from God to fulfill his. She may have ended up with someone good, but maybe he was not God's best choice.

This story is just one of many in the Church who have married for the wrong reasons. They pair up without regard to God's purposes and their role and responsibility in His Kingdom. Many times couples don't involve God until the wedding ceremony. Physical attraction and romance seem to be enough. This is somewhat the norm in most churches—and the reason why Christians have the same negative marriage statistics as unbelievers.

When God paired people in the Bible, He based it on Kingdom purpose, even in the very lineage of His Son Jesus. Each person played a major role that affected His ultimate plan and message to His children. It is vital for anyone who considers marriage to have this correct perspective. The couple must have the same call and destiny to be perfectly suited to each other for the Kingdom and purposes of God.

The only way to achieve that is by letting God be in full control of your life. Stop making things happen. As you keep your eyes on God, and as the one He has for you does the same, eventually you will meet and be together. There is no "spouse-hunting" in God's Kingdom. He'll make it all happen according to His plans and timing. That is exactly what happened with David and me (more about that in Chapter 11).

FOLLOWING CARNAL DESIRES

The Bible contains numerous examples of people who defied God's standards in regard to relationships and paid a heavy price. Samson pursued a wrong relationship with Delilah, a harlot, and lost his strength, the favor of God, his eyesight, and eventually his life (see Judg. 14-16). Esau lost his inheritance, married pagan wives, and fathered children whose descendents became some of Israel's most hostile enemies (see Gen. 25:33-34; 26:34). King David lusted after Bathsheba, slept with her, getting her pregnant, and in the course of trying to cover his tracks, had her husband killed. Although David repented and received forgiveness from God, the physical consequences of his sin afflicted him for the rest of his life (see 2 Sam. 11-12). King Solomon followed the Lord faithfully until he acquired pagan wives and concubines who led him astray (see 1 Kings 11:1-13). Each of these people reaped bitter fruit when they went against God's standards. Why should we assume that it would be any different with us?

I knew a divorced minister who was in his late 50s. Because of his age, he was very anxious to remarry. He kept saying that he was made to marry; so he started dating. He soon hooked up with a divorced Christian woman whom we knew very well. She was slightly younger than him, but she was very strong in the Lord and had been single for a long time. They had been dating for a couple months when he asked me for some counseling. I began by asking him if he had tested to see if their relationship was of God before entering into it. I emphasized how extremely important it was that they both knew for certain that they were God's choice for one another. Otherwise *he was dating someone else's future wife, in a sense.* At first he was shocked, as he had never thought of dating that way, but the more he thought about it, the more it made sense to him.

He suggested to the woman that they separate for a month to pray and seek God's will concerning their relationship. She wanted to be absolutely certain to hear from God and suggested three months instead. He wasn't entirely happy with the idea of a three-month separation but agreed anyway. During that time, the Lord showed them both that they were not meant for each other. He was disappointed because he really wanted to get married. He had trouble surrendering that desire and leaving it in God's hands. He was looking to marriage rather than to God as his source of happiness and fulfillment.

Years later we learned that he continued dating other women with increasing desperation as he was getting older. Finally he got married, only to wind up divorced shortly afterward. His wife left him after only a few months. He was devastated for the first couple of years and kept hoping that she would return. He was miserable because he kept holding on. We told him that he had to let her go and leave her in God's hands. He finally did, and he is now happily serving God in his singleness, letting Him be the One to complete and fulfill him.

I knew another girl who was easy-going but never really fired up for God until she moved with her family to California. She attended Bible school and discovered that her calling was to be a missionary to Africa. Her heart was burdened for the Africans because her church had outreaches there. As she wrote me concerning her life in school, she mentioned that she was getting along really well with her roommates.

When David and I visited her, we were disappointed to see that her roommates were more lukewarm than fired up for God. We were concerned that it would stifle her fire for God; they were more boy crazy and just wanted to have fun. They were more committed to watching the latest movie than to being equipped to serve God. Sure enough, the girl gradually lost her fire and vision for Africa and became lukewarm like her roommates.

She then began dating a guy who was not a strong Christian. He did everything to impress her with his charm and "brand name" clothes. His parents sent him to Bible school hoping to get him more fired up for God. Unfortunately he wanted only to follow his carnal desires. The next thing I knew, the two were engaged.

When they got engaged, they avoided counseling from anyone, even from the leaders of their school concerning their relationship. They just didn't want anyone to disapprove of them or to tell them what to do, so they proceeded with their own plans. Her parents' involvement came at the end, only to prepare for the wedding, but they were not involved in the approval of their relationship. She asked David to marry them, but he graciously declined, as he didn't want to be responsible before God for marrying two people who were not approved by Him and who didn't go through the right process before marriage.

Years have gone by since they've been married, and now they have children; but she lost her vision and fire for God. She still goes to church, but she's empty and unfulfilled, even after she got what she thought would bring her joy and fulfillment.

They reminded me of the Israelites who left Egypt. They kept lusting over what they had "back there" and did not appreciate what God had provided for them, like manna (angels' food) and water from a rock. So while they were still eating what they craved for, God's judgment came upon them.

> But they hastily forgot His works; they did not [earnestly] wait for His plans [to develop] regarding them, but lusted exceedingly in the wilderness and tempted and tried to restrain God [with their insistent desires] in the desert. And He gave them their request, but sent leanness to their souls and [thinned their numbers by] disease and death (Psalm 106:13-15).

People don't realize that when they forget God's goodness and wondrous works they are insulting Him. That is what happens when people get impatient with God. They don't want to wait for His plans to develop. So they make their own plans, insist that God makes them work, and then ask God to bless them. They want their blessings, mate, promotion, and big doors to open *now!*

What causes us to think and act that way? Once we start entertaining those kinds of thoughts and attitudes, it's a clear sign that we have lost our focus and trust in God. When the enemy gets you to doubt God, rather than relying on Him, it is easy to fall into sin. These are the same tactics that he used on Eve (see Gen. 3:1). The enemy wants you to question God's goodness, faithfulness, and ability to provide you with what you need. He wants you to think that God doesn't know what is best for you. And he wants you to take matters into your own hands and make what *you* desire happen. Even in the most perfect environment, where all of her needs and wants were met, the enemy was able to cause Eve to doubt and question God and to fall into sin. So your environment is not what needs to change. It's *you*—your heart, your perspective, your mindset, your will, and your attitudes. When all of those things are on the right track and focused on God, then you can change your own environment.

The right thing at the wrong time is the wrong thing. When you want your blessings badly enough to obtain them prematurely, before God thinks you are ready, God may grant them to you, but His judgment and wrath will also be released upon you because of your persistence in having your own way and not trusting Him. He has wonderful things in store for you, but He has them on a perfect timetable, ready to be released at the proper time and place. *The best things in life are worth waiting for.*

COST OF OBEDIENCE

Do not love this world nor the things it offers you, for when you love the world, you do not have the love of the Father in you. For the world offers only a craving for physical pleasure, a craving for everything we see, and pride in our achievements and possessions. These are not from the Father, but are from this world. And this world is fading away, along with everything that people crave. But anyone who does what pleases God will live forever. Dear children, keep away from anything that might take God's place in your hearts (1 John 2:15-17; 5:21 NLT).

There is a cost to following Jesus. The enemy is quick to reveal the cost of obedience and magnify how difficult, impossible, uncomfortable, scary, and painful it looks if you obey. The enemy will be persistent in telling you, "It's not worth it; this can't be God; take the easier road; you don't need this kind of suffering in your life," and so forth.

The enemy is also as quick to hide the price of disobedience from you, like the lifetime of negative consequences that affect you, those around you, your future, and your career and the way that disobedience robs you and your children of your blessings and godly inheritance. He wants to bind you and have you lose out on God's best by settling for something just good enough, to deprive you of the opportunity to see God work wonders on your behalf.

> *Do not be deceived and deluded and misled; God will not allow Himself to be sneered at (scorned, disdained, or mocked by mere pretensions or professions, or by His precepts being set aside). [He inevitably deludes himself who attempts to delude God.] For whatever a man sows, that and that only is what he will reap* (Galatians 6:7).

Basically we won't get away with deceiving God and others. Whatever we do will catch up to us sooner or later. Disobedience has a higher price tag and causes a much greater loss.

> *Friends, when life gets really difficult, don't jump to the conclusion that God isn't on the job. Instead, be glad that you are in the very thick of what Christ experienced. This is a spiritual refining process, with glory just around the corner* (1 Peter 4:12-13 TM).

Just because it is hard doesn't mean that it's not God's will for you to be there. When you're going through hell, just go through it and do not stop. Don't stay there perpetually. In fact we are commanded to rejoice (see Phil. 4:4). Joy gives you the supernatural strength to go through hell like anesthesia before an operation.

Looking for a "get-out-of hell" card each time you're going through tough times will keep you from maturing and receiving the blessings and the glory that will be revealed after you've passed through the trial. It is never good to make hasty decisions when you are in the midst of a trial. That is when your flesh kicks into high gear to influence your decision. Just stay focused and do not lose sight of what God is trying to bring into your life through it. Obey God, even when it looks impossible and painful at the moment. After it's all over and you are finally reaping your just reward, you'll think, *I'm ready, Lord, for the next one!*

EMOTIONS—UNRELIABLE SOURCES

Emotions constantly change and are unreliable sources of reality. Christians who do things according to their emotions are considered "carnal" because their emotions govern their lives. It is much easier to be led by our emotions because emotion-based living does not require the crucifying of our flesh. It is simply giving free reign to our feelings with no care of the consequences.

Therefore, dear brothers and sisters, you have no obligation to do what your sinful nature urges you to do. For if you live by its dictates, you will die. But if through the power of the Spirit you put to death the deeds of your sinful nature, you will live. For all who are led by the Spirit of God are children of God (Romans 8:12-14 NLT).

Scripture is clear: those who live according to their sinful nature and cater to their flesh can never please God. Although there is a distinction between occasional lapses into sin and a habitual sinful lifestyle, they both can lead to severe consequences. It only takes one lapse into sexual sin to conceive a child or catch a disease and be discredited by the world and the Church. Other sins, such as anger, may not carry these same levels of ramification. Though there is forgiveness for all sin, sexual sins have greater consequences. It is safe to say that such sins should never even be "named among you" (see 1 Cor. 5). The condoning of habitual sexual sins calls into question the genuineness of one's faith.

How many times have we given in to our emotions when it comes to relationships? We've allowed our flesh to tell us what to do, where to go, and how to do it just to satisfy its cravings. Saying *I love you* as a ploy to get temporary pleasure is not practicing Christ-like love.

The grace of God leads us to repentance and deliverance. Often believers tolerate sin and put a "grace" sticker on it instead of dealing with it. Some like to call repentance "legalism" as an excuse for not letting God deal with them. Holiness and spiritual maturity mean learning to live more and more each day in such a way that sin has less and less power over us while the Holy Spirit manifests in us more and more through our pursuit of purity.

As we pursue purity, self-control plays a vital part. Self-control means exercising restraint, and it is one of the fruit of the Spirit (see Gal. 5:22). We cannot do this in our own strength. We need to rely on and get full of the Holy Spirit in order to develop self-control. Acting on emotional impulse demonstrates that we are still bound by our sinful nature. But the more often we let ourselves be guided and controlled by the Holy Spirit when faced with temptation, the more it will become a natural response for us. Perfect practice makes perfect.

It may start out as discipline, but as you keep doing it, soon it will become a delight. And when we delight ourselves in doing everything the Lord wants, we will prosper and have abundant life.

Oh, the joys of those who do not follow the advice of the wicked, or stand around with sinners, or join in with mockers. But they delight in the law of the Lord, meditating on it day and night. They are like trees planted along the riverbank, bearing fruit each season. Their leaves never wither, and they prosper in all they do (Psalm 1:1-3 NLT).

Above all else, guard your heart, for it affects everything you do (Proverbs 4:23 NLT).

God is really emphasizing the importance of guarding and restraining our hearts at all cost. Why? Because: *"The human heart is most deceitful and desperately wicked. Who really knows how bad it is? But I know! I, the Lord, search all hearts and examine secret motives. I give all people their due rewards, according to what their actions deserve"* (Jer. 17:9-10 NLT).

If we don't protect and train our hearts to overcome evil, we will easily abandon God's principles and standards. And if you don't set God's standards in your heart long before you get into relationships, then when you are in a middle of temptation, it will be very easy to compromise and fall into sin (see Ps. 37:31). Make sure that you get it firmly established in your heart and commit to keeping it at all cost (see Prov. 7:1-3).

Those who are dominated by the sinful nature think about sinful things, but those who are controlled by the Holy Spirit think about things that please the Spirit. So letting your sinful nature control your mind, leads to death. But letting the Holy Spirit control your mind, leads to life and peace. For the sinful nature is always hostile to God. It never did obey God's laws, and it never will. That's why those who are still under the control of their sinful nature can never please God (Romans 8:5-8 NLT).

According to this Scripture in Romans, our spirits want to obey God, but not our hearts. The flesh always opposes the spirit. If left on its own, the heart will lead us to compromise and sin, to veering off God's path and believing lies as truth. God said that if we let our sinful nature (emotions/heart) control our mind, there will be death—besides physical death, it could also mean our downfall, a life of misery, frustration, and defeat.

There are many things in life that we do every day despite how we feel, because life and society would not function otherwise. If you stayed home from work every time you simply didn't "feel" like going (mood-wise), what would happen? Before long you would be out of a job. Shouldn't we then do what is right concerning relationships simply because it is right and has terrible ramifications if we don't?

You may think, *I really don't want to sin, but I somehow end up doing it anyway. How do I stop giving in to my flesh?* One thing that I have learned: stop feeding it, and it will eventually die. Starve the flesh, and feed the spirit. Crucify—kill, pull the plug—the flesh and its desires (see Gal. 5:24-25). Stop thinking of things that will cause you to sin; then you won't do them. Don't gratify the flesh by letting your heart and mind go out of control. Don't let in any worldliness, fear, or worry.

As God's children, we need to learn to live beyond our emotions and to not allow them to rule our lives. We must submit our flesh and soul to the spirit, not the other way around. When we let the Holy Spirit have full control over our hearts and minds, it's like pressing the "reset" button on our computer and reprogramming our hearts to do what is right, holy, just, and true. Then we shall have life and peace. Now that's a great promise.

HUMANISTIC APPROACH TO LOVE

What is the meaning of having a *humanistic* approach to love? This is when Christians believe in evolution when it comes to marriage. Evolution, of course, is a theory claiming that everything that exists came about by accident without a Creator. According to the theory, there is no God or Creator, so supreme authority lies with humankind. We do whatever we want to do and answer to no one except ourselves. It is the *que sera, sera* approach to life: whatever will be, will be. In dating and marriage, this translates into the belief that whoever we happen to fall in love with is the "right one" for us.

There are many churches that practice, if not teach, this humanistic approach. They believe that each person has many possible mates to choose from and that you get to decide who is "the one." In this case, we do not need God involved at all, nor do we need to have faith in Him for our mate. All we need is the ability to follow our hormones and emotions and maybe a little bit of intelligence to make it work.

God's "Permissive" Will?

Before you say "I do," it is for your own good and security that you know that you know, from your very core, that the one you are about to marry is God's perfect will for you and not His "permissive" will (if one can actually use that term). I believe that it is either God's perfect will or your will. There is such thing as God's "permissive" will concerning the food we it (see 1 Cor. 6:12), but not concerning marriage. You just have to make up your mind which one you want to choose and live with for the rest of your life—God's choice or your choice?

Why is that so important? If you know that you know beyond the shadow of a doubt, and if you've tested it in every angle to make sure that it's truly from God before you even enter into a relationship (not while you're already in it), then when troubles come later, you will never doubt that the one you married is truly the one God has chosen for you.

With that in mind, divorce will never be entertained as an option to alleviate the pressures and uncertainties of life. You will never have to wonder if you missed it somehow when you begin to see things that bother you about your spouse. You will not want out just because challenges stress you out and weigh you down. The only option that you have when things go wrong is to change yourself and your attitude and to work things out with your spouse. Note that

I did not say to change your spouse (as in changing your spouse's attitudes) or to exchange your spouse for someone else; instead I said that *you must change yourself and your attitude.*

After the wedding and its pageantry, reality will set in, and you will have to face life and its challenges together with the person you committed yourself to. As holy as the sexual act is on your first night together, it's not the most important thing. Marriage is not the celebration of legal sex. It's not being able to file joint tax returns and claim deductions. You now face the challenge of trying to connect your hearts as your bodies connect. How do you connect your past to his? How do you connect the weaknesses in you to the weaknesses in her without causing World War III?

Remember, the Lord said that *"everything will be tested and shaken and only those that are truly His will stand"* (Heb. 12:26-27). Even if you've done everything right from the beginning, you will still go through the fire and various trials, but the difference is that you will make it through because you started it the right way and will continue to apply the same principles throughout your married life.

I've heard preachers say that *God created marriage to kill us* because, ever since they've been married, they've been going through a constant process of dying. So if you're not ready for a lifestyle of dying, then you might want to reconsider marriage, because in order to have a successful marriage, you must be willing and ready to die and feel pain. It takes serious *work and commitment, not just love,* to have a marriage that glorifies God, unlike what the world has seen and experienced. It can be painful to work at marriage, but it is more painful to reap failure, strife, and separation from those we love just because we are too proud, stubborn, or busy to take the time to work at it.

It takes more work to build a godly, wholesome, and happy marriage. But at least you can avoid other unnecessary heartaches when you know that you married the right one. You can go through hell and back many times over and yet still pull through together, because the same God who brought you two together can *keep* you together. You've trusted Him this far to guide you to the right one. You can surely trust Him again to guide you through the rest of your journey together. But there's much greater loss and pain when you choose your own way instead of God's.

I beseech you—take the time to truly find the heart of God and His will before you plan to form and build a relationship with someone. Then your obedience to Him and His ways will cause His blessings to come, not just to you, but also to the seed within you.

LOOSEY GRACEY

Loosey Gracey is a term that I use to describe the mindset of Christians who try to spiritualize or Christianize their adaptation to worldly practices. They think that making something *sound* Christian somehow makes it OK and acceptable. I have seen Christians in churches worldwide who condone dating and label those who are against it "legalistic." These churches may be great in many areas such as faith, worship, even walking in the supernatural, yet somehow they have a blind spot when it comes to dating. Like the world around them, they encourage dating among their youth and other singles, including hanging out with the opposite sex in ways and situations that are unhealthy and can lead too easily to temptation.

Believing in and standing for God's Word, ways, principles, and standards doesn't make one legalistic. I and people who believe as I do about dating are not a bunch of stiff and rigid people who are so into the law of the Word that there's no room for God's grace. Certainly not! We are just setting ourselves apart from the world and pursuing holiness that is from God, the kind that He expects us to have and live as His children. *There's a major difference between living in legalism and living in holiness according to God's standards.* Choosing God's best, doing away with worldly practices and carnality, and trusting God for our mate and future is not legalism. It is biblical.

In Western Europe, and especially in France, for instance, where David and I lived and ministered for 12 years, most of the churches are far behind the United States in teaching and understanding holiness and in being a people set apart from the world, especially among the youth and young adults. From everyday believers and worship team members, to ministers, most tolerate and accept actions such as the wearing ultra mini-skirts and other provocative clothing and even the cohabitation of unmarried couples. They approach the formation of relationships the same way that the world does. In fact, many Western European churches teach extreme "grace," often as an intense reaction to having come out of extreme legalism (although there are still many in Europe who practice extreme outward holiness). The very fact that they go from one extreme to the other shows a major lack of balance.

Either extreme is equally damaging. The solution is to find the proper balance between both.

In 1998, David and I were blessed and honored to lead a six-month revival in France, the longest running revival the country had seen in 50 years. We preached holiness and repentance, and people came to Christ at every meeting. Atheists, Muslims, and people from all walks of life were saved and delivered. Many brought their articles of sin—marijuana pipes, pornography, etc.—and laid them on the altar. This move of God also had many healings, miracles, signs, and wonders. People hungry for God came from all over, including other countries. The glory and power of God were evident.

However, the beginning of the end of the revival came as David and I were deeply troubled at the sight of teenage couples and young adults making out in front of the church, some even right at the front door as people were coming in, as though flaunting their activity. Their behavior struck us as revealing a complete lack of fear and honor toward God.

David immediately began addressing this issue in his preaching. He stressed issues of purity and holiness, such as giving up dating, dealing with lust, avoiding fornication, saving oneself for a future mate, believing that sex is acceptable to God only within the context of marriage, refusing to dress provocatively, avoiding physical and emotional oneness, etc. That same evening, the pastor approached us and told us to stop preaching that message. He informed us that French youth were different from American youth. Because the French have a lot of rejection issues and deep emotional hurts, they need to have relationships with the opposite sex in order to feel loved. He wanted us to tone down what they called our "American" gospel. They generally regard American Christians as a bunch of Puritans who need to loosen up a little bit. (I believe that basically God's standard is too high for them, so it's easier to call it an "American" gospel to justify the lowering of their standards.)

As we discovered later, the reason the pastor spoke to us this way was because his daughter was dating a young man in church and he was coming under conviction. She became angry because she disagreed with our message about dating. Other young people felt the same way, so we were banned from addressing those issues from the pulpit. That is when the fire of revival began dwindling, and eventually God ended the revival.

What happened to that church after a revival of repentance and holiness? The very people who came against God's message on holiness ended up backsliding as they continued in their lusts and sinfulness. They ignored the sin of premarital emotional and sexual intimacy and mistook them for love, believing that they needed them in order to feel whole.

Many pastors in Europe marry couples with little or no premarital counseling. Whatever counseling does occur rarely deals with sin issues, accountability, verification of God's approval of the match, or even the couple's complete readiness for marriage. I asked numerous pastors there if they had ever refused any couples' request to marry them. None of them had. In general, they tend to justify their stance by referring to Paul's counsel in First

Corinthians 7:9: *"But if they can't control themselves, they should go ahead and marry. It's better to marry than to burn with lust"* (NLT).

They assumed that God's approval would come automatically, even though they hadn't checked it out beforehand with God Himself. Doesn't it seem odd and inappropriate in a wedding ceremony to ask God to bless this "holy matrimony" when no one bothered to ensure ahead of time that the union was approved by God (much less whether or not the couple was living a holy lifestyle before the wedding)?

Over the years, we have seen many of these couples divorce, live separate lives, or experience other major marital and relational problems. Yet rarely do they connect their difficulties to their earlier refusal to live by God's standards and do things His way.

THIS IS NOT A TEST

Dating is not a test to see how well we can control ourselves amid temptation. Why put ourselves in a vulnerable situation when we could lose control? Why tempt ourselves, seeing how high we can raise the heat before the flame ignites? This kind of risky behavior does not glorify God and easily leads to a loss of purity and spiritual focus. People have no business being entangled in relationships, demanding another's undivided love and affection, if they're not ready to back them up with a lifelong commitment. Even if people are absolutely ready and prepared to make that commitment, when they make room for sin and compromise, they are doing more damage than good in their relationship.

When we change our attitudes and make pleasing God (first) and doing what's best for others (second) our main priorities in relationships, we'll find true peace and joy. The most indispensable benefit of seeking God and His righteousness above all else and of walking in His ways is knowing that we are pure and blameless before God and others.

> So this is my prayer: that your love will flourish and that you will not only love much but well. Learn to love appropriately. You need to use your head and test your feelings so that your love is sincere and intelligent, not sentimental gush. Live a lover's life, circumspect and exemplary, a life Jesus would be proud of: bountiful in fruits from the soul, making Jesus Christ attractive to all, getting everyone involved in the glory and praise of God (Philippians 1:9-11 TM).

We have to do more than wear bracelets that say, "What would Jesus do?" We are to actually live our lives the same way that Jesus did. The passage above says that we must learn to *"love appropriately."* This means loving each other in a way that is mindful of not causing anyone to stumble or fall into sin, loving in the purest of heart and intentions. It reaches beyond the outward purity. *Loving appropriately* is being pure and blameless in our motives, minds, emotions, and actions. This is the kind of purity that God wants us to pursue. Ask yourself this question when you are in a relationship, *Do I truly want to be responsible to God for ruining and violating someone else's purity and innocence, much less my own?*

Many Christian youth and singles want to stay on the straight and narrow yet continue to practice a lifestyle that tends to pull them in the wrong direction. They must realize that dating like the world will not produce something pure and beautiful. Good intentions are not enough to keep people from trouble and sin. Physical intimacy (including kissing, heavy petting, oral and finger stimulation) without commitment awakens physical, emotional, and fleshly desires that are hard to resist. The Word of God says:

> *It is God's will that you should be sanctified: that you should avoid sexual immorality; that each of you should learn to control his [or her] own body in a way that is holy and honorable, not in passionate lust like the heathen, who do not know God; and that in this matter no one should wrong his brother [or sister] or take advantage of him [or her]. The Lord will punish men for all such sins, as we have already told you and warned you. For God did not call us to be impure, but to live a holy life. Therefore, he who rejects this instruction does not reject man but God, who gives you His Holy Spirit* (1 Thessalonians 4:3-8 NIV).

To "wrong" or "take advantage of" means to rip someone off by raising expectations but not delivering, to arouse a hunger that cannot be satisfied righteously, or to promise something that cannot or will not be provided. People do not escape a lifestyle of sin by doing the right thing only once. The right thing has to be done repeatedly before breakthrough comes. And once breakthrough is achieved, the only way to maintain it is to keep doing what is right until right behavior becomes a lifestyle. There is no "quick fix." Discipline and determination, backed by the power of the Holy Spirit, is the only way. No pain, no gain.

If you've asked for forgiveness for becoming too intimate, did you repent because you really wanted to change and because you were remorseful, or did you simply do it because you got caught? That kind of repentance is not true repentance; God will not listen to it or set you free. That's when you are *flirting with darkness*. You might be enjoying the rush that you get from it now, but wait until that rush fades and you're left alone to suffer immorality's ugly consequences. Perhaps even now you are with child, feeling dirty, guilty, and ashamed.

God is faithful to forgive.

chapter 5

THE DANGERS OF
COUNTERFEIT BONDING

There is absolutely nothing wrong with the desire for intimacy—to love and be loved. God created intimacy. But when we embrace the philosophy of the song that goes, *"Looking for love in all the wrong places, looking for love in too many faces,"*[1] it becomes wrong. God designed this intimacy to be met in Him and then in the context of marriage.

WHAT IS COUNTERFEIT BONDING?

The objective of intimacy is to become one with God as a special bonding occurs—you behold God, and God beholds you. *Bonding* here means the formation of close ties between two beings physically, emotionally, mentally, and spiritually.

He loves us with a pure and everlasting love. Then we respond by loving Him with all of our hearts, minds, souls, and strength (see Deut. 6:5). We become so consumed with Him that each day we want to please Him, obey Him, love on Him, increasingly know

Him and His ways, and just enjoy His presence. When we marry, our intimacy with our spouse should be a mirror of the deeper intimacy that we have with God. But when people endeavor to find intimacy outside of marriage, life becomes complicated. The bonding that they create is counterfeit. *Counterfeit* means a realistic copy of the real in order to defraud or deceive.

Let's say you're a piece of red moldable Play-Doh. You get into a relationship with a blue-clay someone, and you bond and develop ties, mixing blue and red. After some time, you break up with Blue; then Yellow comes along, and you bond together. But after awhile, Yellow doesn't work out and it's over. By now, your beautiful red has turned into a dirty-looking mud color.

With each relationship, the transference of each other's color—souls, spirits, and demons—takes place. Because there is such a mixture of debris left from each person, it is almost impossible to sort out all of the joys, hurts, and baggage that each relationship evokes. This is far from how God designed love and relationship to be. This is definitely not His plan for His children. God did not create our hearts to bond and break again and again. We may think it's easy to get over people and hurts, but it isn't. That is why more and more families are dysfunctional today.

SIGNS OF COUNTERFEIT BONDING

Counterfeit bonding makes people think and feel that "love" is drawing them together, to the point of having great difficulty in separating themselves from the other—even in abusive or unfaithful relationships. The amount of pain felt after a break-up usually corresponds directly to the amount of bonding. When the physical, emotional, or spiritual level of involvement is greater than the commitment level, that is counterfeit bonding.

Dating perpetuates counterfeit bonding. It also affects your relationship with God and your future mate. The atmosphere of dating fuels lust and encourages the gratification of carnal desires. Even if Christians never intend to fall into the trap, they often give in because of the desire for intimacy that God has placed in us—but that is to be reserved for marriage alone.

PHYSICAL BONDING

...Well, it may be true that the body is only a temporary thing, but that's no excuse for stuffing your body with food, or indulging it with sex. Since the Master honors you with a body, honor Him with your body! God honored the Master's body by raising it from the grave. He'll treat yours with the same resurrection power. Until that time, remember that your bodies are created with the same dignity as the Master's body. You wouldn't take the Master's body to a whorehouse, would you? I should hope not.

There's more to sex than mere skin on skin. Sex is as much spiritual mystery as physical fact. As written in Scripture, "The two become one." Since we want to become spiritually one with the Master, we must not pursue the kind of sex that avoids commitment and intimacy, leaving us more lonely than ever—the kind of sex that can never "become one." There is a sense in which sexual sins are different from all others. In sexual sin we violate the sacredness of our own bodies, these bodies that were made for God-given and God-modeled love, for "becoming one" with another. Or didn't you realize that your body is a sacred place, the place of the Holy Spirit?

Don't you see that you can't live however you please, squandering what God paid such a high price for? The physical part of you is not some piece of property belonging to the spiritual part of you. God owns the whole works. So let people see God in and through your body (1 Corinthians 6:13-20 TM).

If we really believed that our bodies are where God lives, would we allow His house to be used for sin? Would we become one with a sinner? If our bodies are God's house, doesn't that mean that God is the final authority in deciding what we should eat or drink and what activities we should be engaged in? Many don't see their bodies in that way; otherwise they wouldn't commit sexual sins, indulge in gluttony, or poison themselves with drugs, alcohol, and tobacco. Our bodies are not our own; the whole package belongs to God. So we don't use our bodies to do what we want to do, especially not to commit sexual sins. Not only do they belong to God but they are also holy and sacred, to be used for God and His purposes only. He owns our bodies and paid a high price to redeem us from sin. Let us not defile them by using them to commit unholy acts.

If you have had sex outside of marriage, you didn't just have sex with one person. Rather, you also had sex with all of their previous partners and with all of their partners' partners, etc. As in the illustration of the Play-Doh, when you have sexual intimacy with someone, you become one with that person (see 1 Cor. 6:16). Numerous sexual partners mean multiplied transference of spirits and diseases. When this happens, you lose the original notion of bonding with one mate for a lifetime, as God originally planned.

Imagine this scenario: a girl is alone with her boyfriend at her place. The lights are dim, and no one is around except them. They are watching a movie together, and soon enough the boy's hand wanders. It starts out on her leg and then moves upward. The girl tries to say "no," but her voice doesn't sound convincing. The more she says "no," the more the boy hears "yes," and in each passing moment the heat intensifies.

Soon they are engaged in an activity that they didn't intend to get into, but when alone together, it was too easy to get caught up in the heat of the moment. She tries to resist, but part of her enjoys the stimulation while another part of her knows that what is going on is wrong.

Before the fire totally explodes, she pushes him away. She doesn't want to go all the way. When the night is over and the boy has gone, she is left alone feeling dirty, guilty, and regretful about what happened. But at this young age, when hormones are raging, she doesn't regret it enough to end the behavior completely, and she plays the same game over and over again. In the back of her mind, she tells herself that she can't give it all up because it feels too good and makes her feel wanted. Wanted, yes; loved, no. The truth is, she feels used but can't admit it. The boy will play the game for only so long before he gets tired of it. He will either keep trying until he succeeds in having sex with her, or he will simply dump her to find an "easier" girl.

What happens if sex actually does take place? That's when excuses arise to justify it: *I know it was wrong, but it just kind of happened.* We didn't mean for it to happen. *Somehow one thing led to another and voila.* A few weeks later, the girl finds out she is pregnant. Now what? Were a few moments of sexual pleasure worth a lifelong consequence? Or if she doesn't give in, and the boy just dumps her, she's now left feeling dirty with a broken heart. Counterfeit physical bonding has taken place and will continue to haunt her.

Many justify fornication because of being "in love" and think that God's OK with it. Yeah, right. Where is that in the Bible? Although they may plan on being married, I believe these people have a distorted definition of love. They are really "in lust." Lust is the enemy's counterfeit for love. Does love from God prompt a guy to have sex with his girlfriend or make out with her when it will only damage her purity, wound her emotionally, and damage her relationship with God? Does love from God motivate a girl to entice and seduce a guy in order to fulfill her emotional need for love and affection?

Lust is to feel a strong desire to have sex with somebody, to have a very strong desire to obtain something or someone. The person can be totally nice and have many other good qualities, but that doesn't justify their lust for you or your decision to yield yourself to them. People want to walk up to the edge of sin, bend over, and look down—most wind up falling into sin because they think they can handle getting too close. They keep their fingers crossed, hoping not to reap dreadful consequences. What does Scripture teach?

Abstain from evil—shrink from it and keep aloof from it—in whatever form or whatever kind it may be. And may the God of peace Himself sanctify you through and through—that is, separate you from profane things, make you pure and wholly consecrated to God—and may your spirit and soul and body be preserved sound and complete [and found] blameless at the coming of our Lord Jesus Christ, the Messiah. Faithful is He Who is calling you [to Himself] and utterly trustworthy, and He will also do it [that is, fulfill His call by hallowing and keeping you] (1 Thessalonians 5:22-24).

Paul's warning to *shun youthful lusts and flee from them is followed by his positive call to aim at and pursue righteousness, or conformity to the will of God in thought, word and deed.* There is no way that you can flee from something that you initially choose to be entangled in—except through the grace of God. Why create an atmosphere for sin if you were not planning on sinning? Why allow yourself to be tempted if you know it's wrong and will regret it afterward?

The Christian world today is being bombarded continually by everything that is against God and His truth, ways, and values. There are so many distractions today that can lead us in the wrong direction. Women are told in direct and subtle ways that they must wear a size 0, have perfectly white teeth, and full lips; while men are encouraged to have nice biceps and triceps and perfectly cut abs. From movies and commercials, to the Internet and billboards, the dominate messages dictate that people need to be romantically and sexually involved to be "normal."

Each day we must make a conscious choice to protect our spirits, souls, and bodies from all of the filth of the world, filling ourselves only with things that are good, wholesome, holy, and praiseworthy, things that will edify and strengthen us in the Lord (see Phil. 4:8). We must go against the flow and do what is right.

In *I Kissed Dating Goodbye,* Joshua Harris writes:

> We can only attain righteousness by doing two things—destroying sin in its embryonic stage and fleeing temptation. How? For me and many other people I know, it has meant rejecting dating altogether. I go out with groups of friends and avoid one-on-one dating, because it encourages physical intimacy and places me in an isolated setting with a girl. Can't I handle it? Don't I have any self-control? Yeah, maybe I could handle it, but that's not the point. God says, Run from anything that stimulates youthful lust. Follow anything that makes you want to do right. Pursue faith and love and peace, and enjoy the companionship of those who call on the Lord with pure hearts (2 Timothy 2:22 NLT). God is not impressed with my ability to stand up to sin. He's more impressed by the obedience I show Him when I run from it.[2]

Why should you put yourself in a situation where the lines become smudged and unclear? Why take the risks? Why surrender to the enormous pressure of temptation when you can easily avoid it by refusing to be anywhere where compromise is possible.

The Dangers of Counterfeit Bonding

We are commanded to abstain from every form of evil. Other translations of the Bible say to avoid every kind of evil. To *abstain* means to stay away from every form of evil, even the appearance of evil. But spending time alone, sharing a room or a house, or going for a long drive or trip with the opposite sex, especially a boyfriend or girlfriend, is not abstaining from evil, much less the appearance of evil.

I've seen Christian singles treat this command with little regard. I have known Christians who see nothing wrong with a girl stopping by her boyfriend's house to spend some time alone (or visa-versa), with letting their Christian daughter's on-again, off-again boyfriend live in their house long-term while their daughter is still living with them, with allowing a Christian girl to share the same hotel room with a non-Christian boy just to save some money, with Christians flirting with the opposite sex just for attention, or even with allowing a Christian boy to hang around the girls' dorm rooms in Bible school as he looks for someone to "minister" to.

I believe that Christians have smudged the lines and have compromised God's standards. We have embraced what would normally be considered taboo in Christian culture. We've mixed our values so much with the world's that it is far removed from the original ideals of Christian living. Instead of affecting and changing our culture, we have allowed the world's culture to influence how we live our lives as Christians.

We must honestly evaluate what we see in our Christian world and admit where we have gone wrong before we can fix it and bring it back to what God intended it to be in the first place. Either we don't preach enough true holiness in the Church (and enforce it) or we just choose to ignore sinful actions, not calling sin "sin" so that it doesn't have to be treated as such. We say, "They're just roommates," when they are really fornicators.

Years ago, when we were living in France, I remember hearing on a Christian preaching program that during Christian conferences and campaigns the pornography channels in hotels go sky high—enormously higher than during the Super Bowl or non-Christian mega-events. It's not normal that same sex marriages, bisexuality, swapping partners, and cohabitation are allowed in some churches today. What happened to holiness and having the fear of God? Something is definitely wrong with this picture!

Once Christian couples have committed counterfeit physical bonding through sexual involvement, which includes heavy petting, foreplay, oral sex, etc., it's very difficult, if not impossible, to hear from God concerning their relationship—whether they should stay together or not, whether it is God's will or not. Sin blocks communication lines with God. Their desire to turn away from their sin and to please God *has* to be greater than their sexual desires.

The sole true motivation that will propel most people to purge the uncleanness of their hearts is the desperate longing for a right relationship with God. If purity is the condition for experiencing God's true love in its highest power, then lust is its satanic opposite with a deceiving and insatiable force. By holding onto lust, believers hinder intimacy with God because sin separates us from God. Deliverance and right standing with God must be our ultimate longing, not the desire to hold onto momentary pleasures.

EMOTIONAL BONDING

Counterfeit emotional bonding happens when you give your heart and emotions to someone who surpasses the friendship level. How does that happen? It happens when two people share deep things with one another—problems, concerns, hurts, even their dreams, personal prophecies, and intimate secrets. Those things should not be shared with anyone who is just a friend or less. If you have this kind of conversation with someone other than a spouse or intended spouse, you've crossed the boundaries of friendship and moved your relationship into something more. Soul ties take place as your souls bond through the sharing of intimate things, even though they are only in the soul realm and not the physical. As time goes by, it could easily lead to physical intimacy since you already feel connected with each other in your hearts.

Some may not have committed sexual affairs, but they have committed emotional affairs. I remember when David and I ministered in Qatar, a small country bordering Saudi Arabia. A Christian Indian woman asked me to pray for her marriage. As I agreed, I asked for specifics concerning her marital problems. She explained that her husband was weaker spiritually and that she wanted her marriage to end because of that. I went to the husband, and he said that he really wanted to save his marriage. I could sense sincerity and also deep sadness coming from his heart.

On the other hand, the wife seemed quite indifferent. I took her aside and felt led to ask if there was abuse or another person. She said that her husband did not abuse her and that he did not have a mistress. But there was another man in her life. I was taken back, especially because she had called her husband the weaker one spiritually. I asked if she had any sexual intimacy with the other man. She said no, but that there was an emotional bond between them. Although there was no sexual involvement, they had committed counterfeit emotional intimacy—*emotional adultery*. This sin is just as dangerous and damaging as sexual adultery.

I strongly advised her to repent for having an emotional affair with another man, to forgive her husband for any offense, and to work things out with him. There is no problem that God cannot help them solve. I counseled about the pain and damage that divorce would cause her 2-year-old son and told her that her husband would do anything that God required of him to save their marriage. I advised that she seek help from her pastors and leaders.

Beyond attraction based on physical appearance is the attraction of shared conversation—the deeper the conversation, the greater the attraction. Communicating past and present hurts and dreams for the future is the principle way that couples form emotional intimacy, which is why that kind of sharing should be reserved only for a relationship committed to marriage. Women are usually the ones with a tendency to be too accessible to men and too susceptible. Because men tend to withhold more, any sign of interest, attention, or concern can easily be mistaken as something more than a friendly gesture.

Sometimes a reverse in roles can take place, as happens with men who can get quite obsessed with women, especially men who experience a lot of rejection and consider themselves as outcasts. When a woman pays attention to them or shows them compassion, they may misinterpret it as a signal of wanting to be more than friends. Little acts of kindness or flirtations can be taken the wrong way. Whether done out of ignorance or not, counterfeit emotional bonding can easily take various forms, such as offering a shoulder to cry on, listening to stories, exhorting and supporting, or being a kindhearted friend.

Many dating relationships have begun with emotional bonding. Regrettably some break up and suffer from intense hurt, betrayal, rejection, abandonment, anger, resentment, unforgiveness, and hatred. These people are so affected by the break-up that they bring these negative feelings into other relationships, even into their marriages. Numerous marriages have suffered or ended in divorce from misplaced anger from past hurts.

Here are some ways to prevent this kind of counterfeit bonding to take place, especially between friends:

- **Boundaries.** Avoid sharing deep, intimate issues such as your problems, concerns, past and present hurts, even your dreams and aspirations, personal struggles, prophecies, and intimate secrets with anyone other than your spouse or intended spouse. Stop someone immediately, but graciously, if the conversation turns intimate. Let the person know that you share those topics only with your spouse.

- **Avoid ministering one-on-one to the opposite sex.** In our ministry, we made it a rule that one-on-one witnessing or ministering must be with the same sex to avoid counterfeit emotional bonding. It's safer that way. While in high school, I witnessed one-on-one to boys and talked about Jesus with all my heart. They would show an interest and made me believe that they really wanted to hear more about Jesus. In reality, they just wanted to go out with me.

If you have counterfeit emotional ties, break them totally off, especially before you enter into marriage with God's chosen one. It is imperative that you break off every soul tie from your past relationships. Eliminate every love letter, picture, gift, and piece of jewelry, and delete every E-mail and digital photo. Let there be no trace of them whatsoever. Break every emotional tie by the power of the blood of Jesus. Let His blood wash over every sin, memory, and tie. When your slate is clean and free, you can get intimate with God, and He will fill your emptiness with His love and presence. Let Him take all of your hurts and turn them into joys. Let Him restore wholeness to you as you allow Him to take over your entire life.

SPIRITUAL BONDING

Counterfeit spiritual bonding can happen so subtly that many are unaware about how they have even fallen into this trap. A strong Christian girl and boy can get spiritually attached when they share intimate spiritual things with one another. As they spend time praying together and sharing spiritual things with one another, without any physical or emotional bonding, their spirits bond and a spiritual counterfeit bonding takes place.

Do not have someone of the opposite sex as your prayer partner. When you pray one-on-one with someone of the opposite sex, especially regularly as prayer partners, you create both a counterfeit emotional and spiritual bond. It is easy to mistake brotherly love, compassion, and even the strong anointing that you feel when you pray and share conversations for romantic love. When a relationship develops, it is easy to misinterpret all those emotions as God putting you together.

Sometimes one of the two feels the romance, while the other doesn't. Great disappointment and hurt result when ties develop outside of a committed relationship that leads to marriage. So beware of having a prayer partner of the opposite sex. You will eventually get hurt when you rely on that person instead of on God for your spiritual sustenance.

REPENTANCE, HEALING, AND RESTORATION

Now I am glad I sent it, not because it hurt you, but because the pain caused you to repent and change your ways. It was the kind of sorrow God wants his people to have, so you were not harmed by us in any way. For the kind of sorrow God wants us to experience leads us away from sin and results in salvation. There's no regret for that kind of sorrow. But worldly sorrow, which lacks repentance, results in spiritual death (2 Corinthians 7:9-10 NLT).

There is nothing that you might have done that His blood can't wash away and forgive. That is the power of His forgiveness. It's available to anyone who comes humbly before Him in true repentance. True repentance requires a true change of heart, mind, emotions, and actions, not just a simple, halfhearted prayer without any intention of a true change of heart.

As unpleasant as your sorrow may feel after being confronted with your sin, I pray that it produces godly sorrow that leads you to repentance and pushes you toward God. Pain can be a good thing because, as we feel the depth of the pain from our sin, the Holy Spirit can do His work in our hearts. We see our trials as opportunities for us to get closer to God and for Him to heal and restore us, not as obstacles that keep us from advancing.

Repent, then, and turn to God, so that your sins may be wiped out, that times of refreshing may come from the Lord. ...They should repent and turn to God and prove their repentance by their deeds (Acts 3:19; 26:20 NIV).

There is hope and redemption for you when you repent. If you ask Him every day for help, He will help you. Never live a day of your life thinking that you can handle life without His help and guidance. Seek out help, healing, and deliverance through your pastors or church ministries. Just make sure that it's the kind of church or ministry that deals truthfully with your issues according to God's Word and standards, not one that tolerates sin and compromise. No matter what you've done, or what's happened to you in the past, God will set you free and heal you.

That's what He did for a friend of mine. She got saved as a child but backslid during her adolescence. She lost her virginity during this time. Then one day she was tired of feeling the guilt and shame because she knew that what she was doing was wrong. So she repented and recommitted her life back to God. Then she asked God to restore her virginity and purity. She believed and knew that God could restore what she had lost in the past. She held on to it and believed that it was done. She got so fired up for God that even now she is still burning hot for Him.

She married the right one God had picked for her. On their wedding night, she bled as they consummated their marriage for the first time as if she was a virgin. God restored her virginity like she believed He would. She wanted the best for her husband, and God saw her heart. She is still happily married with three sons, and the family continually walks in obedience to God. There is joy forevermore for those who forsake their sinful ways, for those whose sins are forgiven and who walk in true liberty. If you've blown it in the past and have seriously repented and have forsaken your sinful ways, God will do the same for you.

If you want to repent and haven't approached God yet, just pray this prayer out loud, and God will forgive and heal you: *Heavenly Father, forgive me for all my sins. Let your blood wash away every sin, guilt, and shame from me. Wash away even the memories of them from my mind. Break and remove all of the counterfeit ties that I have with _____ (say their names), also remove lust, sexual perversion, and every unclean spirit from me. Break the power of my sins off me. By the power of the shed blood of Jesus, which I put on me, I declare that I am no longer bound and under the power of those spirits. I no longer want them in my life. I come out of agreement with every demonic spirit, and they no longer have any power over me, in Jesus' name. I am free by the blood of Jesus. I also put my iniquity on your bruised body so that the spirit of iniquity from my ancestors is totally broken off of me. I renounce the iniquity of _____, and now it's no longer part of me. I ask Your Holy Spirit to create in me a pure and clean heart, and I ask that You would not take Your Holy Spirit from me. Help and guide me to Your truth and teach me all things that pertain to true holiness, godliness, and purity. Teach me how to live and walk blameless and righteous before You and humankind. I commit myself totally to You. From now on I renew my mind with Your Word. I commit to seek help from Your ministering servants and to not try to do it alone. Thank you Lord for your forgiveness and love and for restoring my purity, innocence, and virginity. Fill me now with Your Holy Spirit. Baptize and consume me anew with Your love, glory, and fire, in Jesus' name, Amen.*

If you've just prayed that prayer, you are now forgiven and free! Yeah! Your heart is as white as snow. You're free to live for God with nothing holding you back. The blood of Jesus is strong enough to break the power of your sins off of you and to make you whole and pure again.

He was wounded for our transgressions, He was bruised for our guilt and iniquities; the chastisement [needful to obtain] peace and well-being for us was upon Him, and with the stripes [that wounded] Him we are healed and made whole (Isaiah 53:5).

Congratulations on your new beginning in God!

PROPER STAGES OF BONDING

Relationships involve bonding. The most intimate relationships pass through four bonding stages: social, spiritual, emotional, and physical. Healthy relationships develop by keeping the bonding stages in the correct order. Following is a chart that shows the correct order of these stages (right column), as well as the type of relationship each one represents (left column).

Commitment	Bonding
Friendship	Social Bonding
God-arranged Relationship	Spiritual Bonding
Engagement	Emotional Bonding
Marriage/Covenant Oneness	Physical Bonding

Notice that physical bonding is the *final* stage in this progression. This is precisely where most people get it wrong—including many Christians—because they are caught up in the "dating game." Most enter the physical bonding stage first, which makes it very difficult to bond in other areas. Keeping this progression in proper order makes it much easier to build positive and healthy relationships that honor God and preserve purity and commitment-based relationships that lead to godly and strong marriages.

With revelation comes understanding, and with understanding comes manifestation. Ask the Lord for more revelation and understanding of His Word concerning these things. As we earnestly seek wisdom, He will reveal His mysteries to us, and He will manifest Himself in wonderful ways.

Keep on asking, and you will be given what you ask for. Keep on looking, and you will find. Keep on knocking, and the door will be opened. For everyone who asks, receives. Everyone who seeks, finds. And to everyone who knocks, the door will be opened (Matthew 7:7-8 NLT).

But the key here is what you ask for. We have to get the order right. His Word says, *"But seek for (aim at and strive after) first of all His kingdom, and His righteousness (His way of doing and being right), and then all these things taken together will be given you besides"* (Matt. 6:33). We mustn't seek things first or we'll end up with something we will regret later. Instead, we must seek God, His Kingdom, and His righteousness (His way of doing and being right). As we keep our eyes on Jesus, we can rest assured that He will bring His very best into our lives in His time and way.

ENDNOTES

1. Waylon Jennings, "Lookin' for Love," *The Essentials of Waylon Jennings* (Legacy Records, 2007).

2. Joshua Harris, *I Kissed Dating Goodbye,* (Colorado Springs, CO: Multnomah Publishers, 1997), 95.

chapter 6

LIES SINGLES BELIEVE

There are many lies that single people believe concerning singleness and marriage. Our Western culture and society contributes to these lies. Through movies, television, and modern-day music, singles are told that:

LIE #1—MARRIAGE IS THE KEY TO HAPPINESS

Many single people think, *If only I could get married, then I'll be happy.* But if that is really true, then why are there many unhappily married people? Even in the Church, among ministers, how many married couples do you see living the ultimate marriage? Not very many, I must sadly say.

Intellectually, unmarried Christian men and women know that God loves them and that He has promised to meet all of their needs. But many still wrestle with the feeling that He really is not enough and that maybe, if only they could get married, they would feel happier. But, if marriage is the key to happiness, why is the divorce rate so high?

Marriage was created and designed by God. It's a beautiful thing, but in and of itself, it is not what makes people happy and fulfilled, nor will it cure loneliness. Some of the loneliest people in the world are married people. Many times loneliness is magnified in marriage when a spouse is unable to fill the void. A spouse cannot meet all of our needs because God did not design them for that. He designed our hearts to be cured of loneliness only through Him, through knowing and living for Him.

Real loneliness is experienced not when you are single, but when you realize that you married the wrong person. It's like living in a self-imposed prison—living in the same house, but living separate lives, sharing the same bed, but lacking true intimacy. Is that what singles really want?

One of the reasons people want to get married is their false expectations of marriage. They have misguided notions about marriage and what they can get from it. Marriage is not about finding someone to make us happy. It is more about learning to make someone else happy. It's not about getting as much as it is about giving. It is not about finding fulfillment as much as it is about self-denial and sacrifice.

Whether you're married or not, Jesus is the only One who can truly satisfy, fulfill, and heal, not a husband or a wife. To expect to have your needs met in marriage is to set yourself up for great disappointment. I'm very happily married, and I'm very blessed to have married the one God has chosen for me. Even with all that, Jesus is still the only One who makes me whole and fully satisfied—not my husband. My husband can kiss and love on me all day, but even his best love falls short of the needs that only God can meet.

No man or woman can take the place of Jesus. As a single, if you do not already have an intimate and personal relationship with Jesus, where you are consistently growing in Him and in the knowledge of Him, then I suggest you develop one now. He is the only One who can fill the void in your heart—the void that you think only a "special someone" can fill. God is that special Someone.

Lie #2—I'm 25 years old and still single— something's wrong with me

Society, culture, and traditions of the natural world exert pressure to be married. The ideal of "having someone," whether as a lover or as a spouse, comes from all sides, from family, friends, coworkers, classmates, billboards, and especially media. If you're a teen, or even younger, and you don't have a "boyfriend" or "girlfriend," then you're not cool.

Most movies revolve around romance, even television shows and commercials. I remember seeing a commercial for laundry detergent. At first it showed a couple shown being romantic and sensual in bed. Then the young woman got up and walked away to wash some clothes. I thought, *What does sex and romance have to do with laundry detergent? They must be really getting desperate to sell laundry detergent!* So nowadays you have to be involved in a romantic relationship in order to even enjoy your laundry detergent. What has our world come to?

I believe women suffer more than men when it comes to being

misunderstood for being single. People tend to think that, if a woman is single, it's because no man wanted her, she's too complicated, or she has major issues. But that reasoning is a lie. Nowhere in the Bible will you find that being single is bad, is a curse, or is abnormal. In fact, being single is encouraged and viewed as something very positive and beneficial in the Kingdom of God. Singles are free to know, love, and serve God with undivided attention.

Paul writes:

I want you to be free from the concerns of this life. An unmarried man can spend his time doing the Lord's work and thinking how to please him. But a married man has to think about his earthly responsibilities and how to please his wife. His interests are divided. In the same way, a woman who is no longer married or has never been married can be devoted to the Lord and holy in body and in spirit. But a married woman has to think about her earthly responsibilities and how to please her husband. I am saying this for your benefit, not to place restrictions on you. I want you to do whatever will help you serve the Lord best, with as few distractions as possible. So the person who marries his fiancée does well, and the person who doesn't marry does even better (1 Corinthians 7:32-35, 38 NLT).

Being unmarried is highly regarded in the Bible. Singles need to see singleness through the eyes of God and not through the eyes of the reprobate world. Where we get our perceptions about life makes a big difference—good or bad. It is imperative that we let only God's Word and truth be the principle influence that shapes our perceptions.

As God's children, we are to be a people set apart from the

world with a completely different set of standards.

Don't let anyone think less of you because you are young [or single]. Be an
example to all believers in what you teach, in the way you live, in your love,
your faith, and your purity. But you, Timothy, are a man of God; so run
from all these evil things. Pursue righteousness and a godly life, along with
faith, love, perseverance, and gentleness. Fight the good fight for the true
faith. Hold tightly to the eternal life to which God has called you, which you
have confessed so well before many witnesses. And I charge you before God,
who gives life to all, and before Christ Jesus, who gave a good testimony be-
fore Pontius Pilate, 14 that you obey this command without wavering. Then
no one can find fault with you from now until our Lord Jesus Christ comes
again (1 Timothy 4:12; 6:11-14 NLT).

Life according to God's standards is what we are commanded to
diligently pursue—running from evil practices and following what
is right and good according to God, not according to the world.
God also says to *pursue a godly life*, not a godly wife (or husband). A
godly mate is not to be pursued. Marriage is a gift to be received
from God, not something that we pursue for ourselves, just like
Eve was given to Adam and Rebecca was given to Isaac.

One lady shared her experience with me: *I have struggled with*
the lie that without marriage I have no value, that perhaps something is wrong
with me. Believing this lie has robbed me of the joy of serving others because I
have been so absorbed with my own goals and deprived myself of the content-
ment that comes from serving and trusting God. This life is so short. God has
helped me have an eternal perspective so the sorrows and disappointments of
this world can be happily endured.

The truth: God has promised us everything we need, and if He knows that a husband or wife will make it possible for us to bring greater glory to Him, then He will provide a mate. Contentment is not found in having everything that we think we want but in choosing to be satisfied with what God has already provided.

Hold tightly to the eternal life that He has given you and not to the temporal desires and lusts for a mate. Obey God's commands with all purity. When you do that, you will become complete and whole as a single person (with nothing missing or lacking); such wholeness is possible only when you pursue and live for Him and Him alone.

LIE #3—SINGLE MEANS INCOMPLETE

Some people believe that they are not a "whole person" if they are single. They believe that they need another person to make them "complete." They believe that a successful marriage is a 50-50 proposition—two incomplete individuals who together will make a "whole" person. That is a major lie!

What a way to put strain in a marriage when each person depends on and takes from the other in order to feel whole. If one or both of them entered marriage empty, with a constant need to be filled, they will eventually exhaust each other. When selfishness is the core, problems will erupt.

God did not design marriage to connect to incomplete people. From the very beginning, it was one whole individual plus another whole individual who were joined together by God. Adam was whole when God created him, and he did not express feelings of loneliness or incompleteness. He was complete in God and was busy doing what God had him do.

It was God, not Adam, who decided that he should not be alone and that he should have a helper (see Gen. 2). In fact, Adam was oblivious; he was not even informed, nor did he ask for it, nor did he manipulate or demand it happen. God simply put him to sleep and took a rib from him and created Eve. God presented Eve to Adam, just as Rebecca was presented to Isaac.

God is the only One who can complete us. We find our wholeness in Him. He is waiting with open arms. "Single and satisfied" is the right attitude.

LIE #4—SINGLE MEANS ALONE.

"A man who has friends must himself be friendly" (Prov. 18:24a NKJV). Chances are, if you don't have friends, you may not be friendly. In order to have friends, you must first learn how to be friendly and how to be a friend. Begin to reach out to others.

Loneliness comes from not understanding who you are in God and from being afraid or too proud to make close friends. Perhaps you have put walls around you because of hurts in your past. You push others away so as not to be hurt again. Open up and let others into your life.

On the other hand, there are those who fear being alone and who need to be constantly surrounded by people; otherwise they get depressed. Without Jesus, there is a void in our hearts. Filthy things have filled our hearts, and they need to be removed. We must submit ourselves to God and give Him all of our hurts and burdens. In exchange, He will fill our hearts with His love, joy, and peace. Don't seek out a person to fill the void. Find your wholeness in Him, and you will never feel empty again.

Sometimes singles who struggle with loneliness have not yet discovered their place in the Body of Christ. Singles, you are not alone. You are part of the wonderful family of God. You are called to function and use your life and gifts to operate within the broader structure of the family of God. You have an obligation to families within the Body of Christ. You carry a responsibility for the lives and marriages of others, for their children and grandchildren, to pray for, encourage, support, and invest in them. One of the most valuable influences on your life and one of the most rewarding investments you could have as a single is time spent with families. Seek out families to be part of, to love and serve, with whom you can grow, pray, play, and worship.

Regularly involving yourself with families safeguards against selfishness. There is no better preparation for marriage and training for those who will marry one day than this.

And let us not lose heart and grow weary and faint in acting nobly and doing right, for in due time and at the appointed season we shall reap, if we do not loosen and relax our courage and faint. So then, as occasion and opportunity open up to us, let us do good [morally] to all people [not only being useful or profitable to them, but also doing what is for their spiritual good and advantage]. Be mindful to be a blessing, especially to those of the house-hold of faith [those who belong to God's family with you, the believers]" (Galatians 6:9-10).

In God's infinite wisdom, He will choose exactly the right combination of individuals whose strengths and weaknesses will help mold you into who He made you to be. Look for opportunities where you can be a regular blessing to a family that God puts into your life, such as attending children's sporting events or dance recitals, running errands, helping with laundry and ironing, shopping, walking the dog, cooking a meal, etc. Both you and the family can offer each other mutual friendship, love, care, support, prayer, accountability, and counsel. Singles can offer strong spiritual reinforcement to the training of the children given by the parents. You can also help parents have time alone as you care for their children. Parents can also offer you time with their family so that you won't feel alone. Everyone benefits when singles are blended into family life.

This integration provides singles with perception, help, encouragement, counsel, and protection in their walk with God. In a family environment, singles witness firsthand the blessings of obeying God's will for the home and the negative effects of disregarding it. Regular in-depth involvement with families also helps eliminate any unrealistic concepts of marriage and parenting.

Singles should not be afraid to reach out to families. Being with a family is a lot of work, but it is also a great blessing. It is a big responsibility, which requires commitment to live the kind of life that glorifies God. It could mean changing your routine so that you can be available to meet their needs. The bigger the investment you are willing to make on behalf of others, the bigger the fruits will be.

LIE #5—GOD HAS MANY FOR ME TO CHOOSE FROM TO MARRY

This is a humanistic approach to marriage, which does not require faith and trust in God and His divine provision. I believe that, since without faith it is impossible to please God (see Heb. 11:6), if people get to choose and have many to choose from, then we wouldn't need God or faith to obtain a mate. There'd be no reason to trust Him for such a provision.

Shouldn't we be different from the world? Doesn't God have a more perfect plan than to leave it all up to us with our limited knowledge and flawed sense of judgment? Without God's involvement, we are well capable of making mistakes and misjudging hearts, characters, and intentions. How then can we let the choosing fall to us and not to God?

There are no Scriptures on which to base the "many" theory, as each time God sets up a marriage, He chooses one specific person to be the perfect match for the other. There was never a second or third choice. That is why marriage and singleness are gifts from God. *"Every good and perfect gift is from above, coming down from the Father of the heavenly lights, who does not change like shifting shadows"* (James 1:17 NIV). So if marriage is a gift from God, shouldn't the choosing and giving of that gift come from Him?

When God made Eve and gave her to Adam to be his wife, God

did not create Sally, Brenda, and Steve too. God chose Eve to be the only one suitable for Adam and for the calling and purpose that they had together as a couple (see Gen. 2:18-25). Likewise, with Isaac and Rebecca (see Gen. 24) there were no other choices but her alone.

God is actively involved in guiding the whole process of finding His choice of mate: the timing, the how, and even the marriage itself. We'll never cease to need God's involvement or to use our faith and trust in Him for everything in our lives, like our calling, our children, our ministry, where we live, when we make life changes, and so forth. It's all part of being His children.

It's not about marrying the perfect person, but marrying the one perfectly suited for you, which only God, through His omniscience, could possibly know. Only He can choose perfectly in order to match the calling that He has placed on your life. It goes beyond compatibility and romance. Being married to the one whom God has chosen *does not* make life free from troubles, but it does avoid the question: *did I marry the wrong one?* Marriage takes commitment, humility, unconditional love, forgiveness, a lot of hard work, and dying to self to make it work and last.

And just like any gift that God gives us, we must *be good stewards.* I don't blame God if the car that He blessed me with broke or ran out of gas. It is just part of maintenance and my responsibility for what He has entrusted me with. Since God is the foundation, from the very beginning and core of the relationship, and since only faith and trust in Him brought it about, it also takes God's provision and our faith and trust in Him to make the marriage work and last.

I need to point out the abuse regarding this issue. Sometimes people tell the person of their fancy that "God" showed or told them that he or she is the one for them, even though it's simply a figment of their imagination or a result of lust. I personally was told by many men that God had showed them that I was "His choice" for them. I simply responded that God had never showed that to me or that it was not God but just their carnal desires and that what they really had was a lust problem. Whatever vision they claimed came from God was just their own fantasy. The voice they heard was their flesh—that is when it gets dangerous.

You have to use discernment and wisdom to deal with people like that. Do not be fooled. Follow protocol and put it to test, then don't waste your time. End the matter before something false and deceptive starts to form. Always have parents or leaders with whom you can share these things for your own protection.

Another excuse that people use to prove that there is more than one mate for us is our free will. God has given us free will. He did not make us robots. That is why it touches His heart when we surrender our God-given free will to His. Our will is in the soul realm, controlled by our heart, which is deceitful and cannot be trusted (see Jer. 17:9). But our will is dysfunctional on its own. Only when we *yield* our will to God's can we make right or godly choices.

I take joy in doing Your will, my God, for your instructions are written on my heart. May Your gracious Spirit lead me forward on a firm footing (Psalm 40:8, 143:10 NLT).

Therefore do not be vague and thoughtless and foolish, but understanding and firmly grasping what the will of the Lord is (Ephesians 5:17).

Even Jesus is a perfect example of surrendering His will to God when He was in the garden of Gethsemane. Just before He was about to be crucified, He said to the Father, *"Let not My will, but Yours be done"* (see Matt. 26:39). He could have chosen not to go to the cross, but He did not give in to His flesh just because it was difficult and painful. He surrendered His free will to do His Father's will instead.

For the joy set before Him, He endured the cross (see Heb. 12:2). He saw beyond His present situation—a glimpse of the future, the consequence of His obedience. That gave Him the joy and the strength to go forward. Likewise, when we get a glimpse of our future with the mate God chooses for us and see how His perfect plan unfolds and brings glory to Him, we can endure any hardship that comes with the whole process.

The Scriptures above teach us to earnestly desire to do the will of God in our lives. We are to understand and firmly grasp what the Lord's will is for us. It sounds clear to me that *we have a responsibility to seek out and know for ourselves what the acceptable and perfect will of God is for our lives.*

Surely God cannot force us to choose His will when it comes to our mate. It is our choice to choose His will over ours. We get to choose His best over what we think, in our carnal and limited minds, is the best. His is the better choice. That is why I strongly encourage people to not make good choices, but only *God choices.*

Trust in the Lord with all your heart; do not depend on your own understanding. Seek his will in all you do, and he will show you which path to take. Trusting oneself is foolish, but those who walk in wisdom are safe (Proverbs 3:5-6; 28:26 NLT).

God says to not trust in our own judgments or in ourselves, but to trust only in Him and to seek His will in all that we do. When we do so, He assures us that He will direct our every step and that we will be safe. Now that's a good deal!

chapter 7

SINGLE FOR GOD

Just as cholesterol coats the arteries and restricts the flow of blood in our physical bodies, so too neglect of God's presence will harden our hearts and clog our spirits, restricting the flow of God's Spirit to us. The enemy comes to distract us. The world calls and entices us. There are multitudes of things that demand our attention; but above all, our flesh draws us back from the Lord and insists on being catered to.

We must decide! We must activate our will. Our problem is not our geographical location or our circumstances. It is us! We need to return to the secret place of intimacy with our Lord. As we do this on a consistent basis, God will restore us, and the flow of His Spirit will return.

We need to come to Him for He longs to be in deep communion with us. God has great things for us to do and to have. He came to remove every hindrance and stumbling block. Out of our consistent intimacy with Him, new things will break forth. He will birth His destiny and purpose into us and through us. He wants to father us.

Jesus is saying: *I don't come into your troubles. But I come close enough so that you can step out of your troubles and come My way.* He meets us halfway so that we can get out of our boat and meet Him. Imagine what we can do through Him when we begin to do things His way.

DATING VS. COMMITMENT

If you do not have an established relationship with your church leaders or if you are not a member of a church, then you are nowhere near being ready for a relationship, nor are you establishing a good and growing relationship with God. If a strong and growing relationship with God is not your priority, then how can everything else in your life be in line with Him? How can you be certain that what you are doing with your life is part of His plan for you if you are not close enough to Him to hear His voice?

This is what I call "dating" God. This describes those who have asked Jesus to be their Savior, but who have not truly made Him the Lord of their lives. Basically, they still do their own thing, living their lives as they see fit—being their own "lord." Their relationship with God is as superficial as dating since they have no true commitment to God. They spend time with Him only when they need His help. But when they don't need Him, they dump Him for another lover. They pick and choose what they want to believe and practice in His Word. They think they have their own deal with God, but there is no depth in their relationship or in their knowledge of Him. That is what it means to date God.

Only someone totally committed and spiritually married to Him, who has an on-going intimacy and relationship with Him, can be totally submitted to Him and His ways. Therefore, a committed Bride is the sole person who can carry His name. When you are only dating Him, you can't carry His name. There is no commitment—just a passing fling or "sentimental gush" centered on what you can get from Him. But only those who are truly committed to Him are His. Not only do they get to carry His name, but they also have the rights to all of His benefits—medical, dental, financial, and material, as well as spiritual riches and emotional and mental wholeness. A dating relationship doesn't have those privileges.

So before you contemplate getting involved in a relationship—if you want the benefit of having the best kind, without any regrets or shame or any negative ramifications—I strongly advise you to first and foremost get your priorities in the right order by making sure that you have a genuine and ever-growing relationship with and commitment to Jesus Christ. Make sure that God has not taken the backseat in your relationship and that everything in your life revolves around Him. Let Him be your number one pursuit in life.

As you do that, find a church that practices what you believe to be the true Church of God and lives what the Bible says. Become a member of that church and develop good and close relationships with the pastors, leaders, and the people there. You will know that it is God leading you when you sense a strong divine connection in the spirit with the pastors and leaders and when you sense in the spirit that this is where God wants you to grow in Him. How can you faithfully commit and submit to God if you can't faithfully and seriously commit to a church and submit to your pastor? How can you call yourself a true child and disciple of God if you never let anyone teach, disciple, and guide you on a personal level? Furthermore, how can you commit and submit your life to a husband or wife?

The way we treat the spiritual leaders in our lives reflects the way we treat God Himself. There are no lone rangers in God's Kingdom. *"He who willfully separates and estranges himself [from God and man] seeks his own desire and pretext to break out against all wise and sound judgment"* (Proverbs 18:1).

How can you successfully become like Christ if you are going about Christianity on your own, without anyone teaching you anything? That is not how He designed Christianity to be. It is similar to birthing a baby into this world and then allowing him to feed himself and care for himself. The baby will die if he doesn't get the proper care and environment. You will die spiritually if you expect to do it all on your own. Then you will return to where you came from—to the darkness of the lost world.

You must make a choice. Make your faith an eternal commitment, not just a passing relationship. As you draw closer to Him, He will draw closer to you. Just as in physical exercise or marriage—*you get what you put into it.* Live to know Him more and to make Him known. Let your life be totally His, and let Him take full control of it, like it says in His Word:

I have been crucified with Christ [in Him I have shared His crucifixion];
it is no longer I who live, but Christ (the Messiah) lives in me; and the life
I now live in the body I live by faith in (by adherence to and reliance on and
complete trust in) the Son of God, who loved me and gave Himself up for
me (Galatians 2:20).

In this verse, we get the full picture of the kind of life that we ought to live after our born-again experience. It is a continually surrendered life to Jesus, not a one-time experience. It is a new life lived by faith in Jesus—in which we entrust our whole life to Him and constantly depend on Him. Our life is no longer ours, but it is His for eternity—to be lived according to His will as we obey and please Him for the rest of our days. That is what it means to be a child of God. Only when we live our lives in that way will we get to experience for ourselves the fullness of what it is like to be His.

It is an amazing life and experience! I can testify of His goodness, love, and faithfulness. God always rewards us with much more than what we sacrificed in obedience to Him. He is not just the greatest God, but He is also the greatest Dad anyone can ever have!

As you learn to hear His voice and know His ways, it is easy to know whether you are on the right track. As you develop sensitivity to His voice and a heart that longs only to please Him, He will guide your every step. He is always there to pick you up whenever you fall. He gives you the strength that you need to do what is right. He always rewards every sacrifice that you make in order to do His will. What a great and loving God we have and serve! Let Him be the One to guide you through life. Find your wholeness in Him and you will be the most fulfilled. If marriage is what He wants to give you as a gift, trust Him to do it supernaturally as your personal Matchmaker. It is well worth the wait.

IMPORTANCE OF INTIMACY

Isn't it reassuring to know that God has great things in store for us? His thoughts and plans for us are always good. We can fully trust Him with our lives. Intimacy with God is what we truly need whether single or married—it's the only way to find true happiness and fulfillment. For those who struggle in this area, let me stir your hunger and desire to have such a deep intimacy with the true Lover of our souls.

When Jesus' love is first awakened in us, He draws us to different stages of His love. The first stage is one of "first love," where He introduces us to His awesomeness. The second stage is one of "fiery love," where He expresses a strength that makes us feel as though we can conquer the world. The third stage is one of "covenant love," where He invites us into His sweet communion and reveals His commitment to us. And the fourth stage is one of "desperate love," where we long for His presence and desire to stay there forever.

Sometimes we're so full of ourselves that Jesus has a hard time getting into us and through to us. That's when He permits us to have what we adamantly wanted and, as a result, suffer the consequences and go through wilderness times. Just when everything seems to be falling apart, He reaches out to us once again. He wants us to lose sight of ourselves in order to gain more of Him.

The Bible is full of examples of men and women who lived in His presence. For Abraham, it was much more than a trip across the landscape to a promised land of abundant provision and blessing. His was a journey of faith that led to intimacy with God (see Gen. 12-25). Should it be any less true for us modern-day spiritual travelers?

When things get shaky and when doubt and fear arise, we begin to see that our spirits are willing, but our flesh is weak and that we're easily drawn away from Him. The cares of this life and the things of the world try to entice and seduce us, but He won't let us go. He is persistent and continues to pursue us. We wander into His presence for brief moments of divine inspiration and then step back out. We settle for occasional encounters with God instead of living daily and constantly in His presence.

We must come to the place where we're no longer content with just a glimpse of His presence. It doesn't matter whether you're a student, doctor, teenager, minister, grandpa, divorcee, plumber, or single parent—we have to be in His presence and dwell there continually. It simply requires our complete surrender to His will to know that we can trust Him with our future.

We shouldn't drift through life like rudderless ships, hoping that we'll stumble upon God's will and purpose for us. Obedience is the only way to get to that place of blessing and rest. Peace can finally enter our spirits as we let go of our security blankets and leave our comfort zones. We may have our own free will to determine our own future, but why not let Him decide that for us. His ways are better and higher than ours (see Isa. 55:9). If we claim to be His children and disciples, then we need to be obedient—there are no other options.

SINGLENESS IS A GIFT FROM GOD

Sometimes I wish everyone were single like me—a simpler life in many ways! But celibacy is not for everyone any more than marriage is. God gives the gift of the single life to some, the gift of the married life to others (1 Corinthians 7:7 TM).

There is no greater Giver than God. He loves to give good gifts to His children. So when God gives us a gift, we are to receive it with thankfulness and joy. He does not give like some friends or relatives during the holidays—when you receive something of no use but politely accept it. God is the best Giver. We can trust His judgments; whatever He gives us is tailor-made to fit us perfectly.

Singleness is a gift from God just as much as marriage is. Neither one is better or worse than the other. Each one has its own joys, advantages, responsibilities, struggles, and pain. Paul cautions us: *"Yes, each of you should remain as you were when God called you. Each of you, dear brothers and sisters, should remain as you were when God first called you"* (1 Cor. 7:20,24 NLT). The point is not the marital status or station in life, but rather choice to live in that state in union with God. So do not seek to have a gift that God has not chosen for you. What is the most important is that, whether married or not, you are in the will of God. Be what God purposed you to be. It may not always look the same. God might send the winds of change your way and surprise you with another gift. But no matter what, let *His* will, not yours, be done.

SINGLE—WHOLE AND COMPLETE

What does being *single* mean—being separate, unique, and whole. God likes uniqueness so much that there are no two snowflakes alike. There are no two human fingerprints that are identical. He created each of us unique and whole.

"So you also are complete through your union with Christ, who is the head over every ruler and authority" (Col. 2:10 NLT). He didn't say that you're complete once you're married. He says that we're complete when we are *one* with Christ. Marriage does not change your wholeness. Even when you marry, you are still a single individual—whole, unique, and complete—just as you were before you married. That's why marriage is not the ultimate goal that God has for you. He wants us to find our completeness and wholeness in Him.

Singles need to work on being whole and deal with the issues that they think marriage would solve. If you lack wholeness as a single, you'll lack wholeness as a married person. If you have problems with lust or anger, you'll have that same problem married. Singles need to ensure that values and standards are well established; otherwise they are easy prey for the enemy.

Build yourself on the Rock, Jesus Christ, and set your feet on the solid ground of His Word so that the pressures and temptations of life won't move you, shake you, or cause you to fall. Until you are truly whole as a single, you are not ready to marry. Marriage will be a terrible experience for you and your spouse. Instead of striving to be married, strive to be truly single and complete in God. Being whole as a single is the very foundation, not just of marital relationships, but of all relationships. *A relationship is only as good as what you put into it.*

Whole people attract whole people because they don't sense the other person constantly pulling on them. Instead of taking, they are constantly giving of themselves. It's a reciprocal giving to each other—*not* a "you give and I take" relationship. Only two complete people can make a complete union because each one is whole enough to want to give to the other. A successful, godly marriage is a by-product of two people being successfully single.

People shine best when they are in the center of God's will. If God's will for you is on the right side, but you keep walking on the left, then all you'll be hearing and getting from God are words to get you back on the right track before anything else. Until you get to that state of true singleness (wholeness), you are not ready to be married. You are better off alone.

UNDISTRACTED DEVOTION

Singles need to be content with friendships. Without marriage commitments, there is ample time and energy to pursue and deepen a relationship with God, develop godly character and God-given gifts, prepare diligently to be a godly and well-equipped wife or husband, serve Him in church or in other types of ministry, and totally focus on fulfilling God's call. God clearly told us the secret to success and a life full of His blessings. *"But seek [aim at and strive after] first of all His kingdom and His righteousness (His way of doing and being right), and then all these things taken together will be given you besides"* (Matt. 6:33).

It's so clear, yet many Christians miss this simple truth and don't apply it in their lives. Our priorities need to follow the godly advice in Matthew 6:33. Train your heart to know Him intimately, to love Him more than anything or anyone, and to serve Him selflessly out of love and gratitude for all He has done for you. Build your trust in Him—we have a long journey, and we need to trust our Father more than ourselves. His Word says that you have every reason to expect the best from Him because of His attributes, because of who He is (see James 1:17), and He never changes. Just don't forget to give Him your best in return.

We can't forget that God has given us a mandate to fulfill and that we're to carry our cross and follow Him. *"Anything I wanted, I would take. I denied myself no pleasure. I even found great pleasure in hard work, a reward for all my labors. But as I looked at everything I had worked so hard to accomplish, it was all so meaningless—like chasing the wind. There was nothing really worthwhile anywhere"* (Eccl. 2:10-11 NLT).

It is a faith walk! Never doubt Him, even during the hardest times when He's purging you. Keep trusting Him. If our longing is for Him, then we will be eternally fulfilled. But if we hope for the perfect mate, the perfect church, or for selfish gain, then our hopes will be deferred. Those things are lesser hopes, lesser loves. Only Jesus is the ultimate!

YOUR SINGLENESS IS FOR GOD'S SERVICE

Singleness is a gift from God for His service. Singles cannot do whatever they want whenever they want and answer to nobody. Christian singles have Christ as Lord of their lives. He owns all of us because He bought us with the priceless cost of His own lifeblood—we owe Him everything. As Lord, His Word is law; it is not open for negotiation. The only option is obedience. Set yourself simply to hear and obey.

> *Indeed, I have been crucified with Christ. My ego is no longer central. It is no longer important that I appear righteous before you or have your good opinion, and I am no longer driven to impress God. Christ lives in me. The life you see me living is not "mine," but it is lived by faith in the Son of God, who loved me and gave Himself for me. I am not going to go back on that* (Galatians 2:20 TM).

Yield yourself to God and let His plan, not yours, be fulfilled. Leave your hopes and dreams at the foot of the cross and focus on living your whole life for Him. Then He will take care of the hopes and dreams that are in your heart. Whatever is from Him will come to pass in His timing. And whatever is not from Him will remain dead and better off forgotten.

Don't wait to do the things that God has put in your heart. Maybe He's given you a desire for missions or a burden for a certain country or people group. This isn't the time to put that on hold so that you can pursue your desire for a mate. The desire for a mate could be the very thing that hinders you from what God wants you to do. God planted in you the desire for those things to propel you toward your destiny in Him. Get busy doing what God has called you to do. Make the Kingdom and righteousness of God your priority, and He will take care of the rest. Everything that pertains to your future is His responsibility, not yours. Your responsibility is to simply obey Him in everything that He asks you to do. Take care of His house, and He will take care of yours. Focus on being a blessing and on being the person God has called you to be, and everything else in your life— like getting married—will fall into place.

STEPS TO WHOLENESS

Here are some steps to take to help you make adjustments in your life that will prepare you to live fully as you journey with God toward your destiny:

1. Abandon dating

Make a conscious decision to abandon dating and all worldly practices for good, and instead adapt God's way of finding a mate. Choose to let God be your Matchmaker. Rely on and trust in Him concerning your future, knowing that He has planned what is best for you. Commit to living a life consecrated and set apart for Him and His purposes.

2. Cultivate your self-worth and identity in Jesus

Since marriage is not the key to your happiness and fulfillment, you must focus and cultivate your self-worth and identity in Jesus, rather than in others. Find your wholeness, contentment, fulfillment, and completion in Him alone. Know who you are in Christ and get deeply rooted and grounded in His Word, truth, and love.

Devote this time to developing godly character and your gifts, and use them for God. Use this time to also prepare yourself for marriage in all areas of your life—spiritually, emotionally, mentally, financially, vocationally, and domestically.

3. Allow God to heal and restore you from past hurts

While you are single, it is the perfect time for healing and restoration so that you may be more effective in His Kingdom. Seek help, healing, and wholeness from your church and other ministries that help in this area. Edify and fortify yourself in Jesus.

4. Seek God for your call and destiny

Find your destiny in God. Don't waste your time doing things that don't lead you toward or help you in your calling. Don't waste your time, emotions, and money on distractions that sway you from your destiny in God. Actively seek what God's will is concerning your life and then prepare yourself for it.

5. Devote your time, abilities, and energy to serving Christ

Whether you know exactly what your call is in God or not, start learning and practicing servanthood by serving a ministry with your time, abilities, and energy. Start with a ministry that has greatly blessed and impacted your life or your local church. Even when God gives you your own vision of what you will do for Him in the future, you still need to take the time for proper training and mentoring before you actually fulfill yours. This is the best way to learn about ministry.

I learned that when you lay down your own vision, and serve someone else in theirs, you will reap it back when the time comes for yours. This also provides you with the covering that you need so that you are not left alone to learn about God's ways and fight the battles that come. You will be better off learning from someone who is already successful than going it alone and making mistakes and potentially hurting others. Also, the only way to learn to be an authority is by learning to submit to one. That covering will go a long way when the battles come.

6. Become part of a family

Many singles get caught in the trap of self-seeking and self-fulfillment instead of devoting their lives to furthering God's Kingdom. It is so easy to concern yourself with nothing else but yourself, tending only to your own needs and wants and forgetting about caring for others. You are free from the responsibility of taking care of a family, so this is easy to do.

However, as mentioned previously, the greatest joy is found in giving yourself to meet the needs of others. You are not placed in this world to be content or to fulfill yourself, but to love and serve the Lord with all of your heart. So get involved in serving and caring for a family. Find out the needs that they may have that you can commit to meet. God will reward you for serving others in this way. This will also keep you from being secluded and from feeling lonely.

7. Cultivate wholesome and godly friendships

This is the time to cultivate wholesome and godly friendships with fellow Christians without getting romantically involved with anyone. This will aid you in fighting loneliness. The Bible says in

Proverbs that there is safety in numbers (see Prov. 11:14). So guard your heart as you pursue godly friendships by avoiding spending time alone with the opposite sex and avoiding counterfeit bonding with them. Don't look at them as potential mates, but strictly as brothers and sisters in Christ. Establish godly boundaries and standards for yourself to keep you from temptation and from compromise. Know the limits of your conversations and time together—what you should share and how long you should spend time with friends.

8. Seek God's will concerning your future mate

Settle in your heart that you will let God alone be your Matchmaker—the only One who chooses your future mate. Leave the choosing, giving, and timing to Him. Die to your desires and flesh and learn to trust Him and to wait patiently. In His appointed place and time, if it is His will for you to marry, He will make it happen without any effort on your part.

GLORY BRINGS CHANGE

Just as our Father is the Creator, so are we in a sense. He has given us the power, through the words we speak, to create or destroy life. God wants us to create our own atmosphere of glory in which we can be going through hell but somehow not act or even smelling like someone in hell. We do not let our circumstances overwhelm us. We set our affections on things above, and not on things below. As we stay in this atmosphere of glory, we actually call forth and create our breakthroughs and miracles through praise and worship, obedience and holiness, and speaking God's Word over ourselves and our situations. We will never feel like we are lacking or missing out in life in this atmosphere. Our perspective begins to change; whether single or married, we change our mindset and conform more to God's ways.

When we are in the presence of God—in the glory—everything changes, because God's glory brings change. Then the changes that take place in our lives brings more glory from Heaven to us. It's a beautiful cycle: we sow glory upward to Heaven, and then Heaven sows glory back down to us. Doing that accelerates everything else in our lives because the glory also brings acceleration. Whatever seeds we've sown will be reaped at an accelerated pace.

This is a particularly significant development for singles. Singleness takes on a whole different meaning. As a single, you can now see that your singleness as a precious gift from God that you are stewarding in the present. Your mind starts to think of a thousand awesome things that you can do for God as a single person. You are actually ecstatic about it and eager to get things going in your life for God. For example, with no family to tie you down, you might consider short- or long-term mission service abroad or even seek employment based on where you believe God wants you to live and serve.

"Finally, brothers, whatever is true, whatever is noble, whatever is right, whatever is pure, whatever is lovely, whatever is admirable—if anything is excellent or praiseworthy—think about such things" (Phil. 4:8 NIV). The mind is the avenue to the soul, and the enemy wants to destroy it. God's infinite love, creativity, anointing, revelation, wisdom, power, and glory will

flow through our thoughts if we will do as He says. Our God is well able to cleanse our mind, to renew it, and to erase the filth. He is well able to cleanse our thought life, even of the filthiest thoughts. But we must choose to do right daily, moment by moment.

We must exercise discipline in order to maintain what He has just cleansed and renewed in us. This means continuing to make the right choices, even when everything in us rebels against it. That is true obedience—one right choice at a time. At any given moment, progress may seem slow, but imagine the positive change that would result from a lifetime of right choices. Imagine where those right choices could lead us in a few years, or ten, or twenty. One thing is for sure: a lifetime of right choices leaves no regrets.

Radical obedience is the key that will propel you to your destiny in God. Extreme obedience will bring you to the next move of God. You see, obedience is cumulative, and so is disobedience. Your present is shaped by your accumulation of obedience and disobedience in the last 20 years or so. If you don't want your future to be just a continuation of your present or to even get worse, then you have to decide to make some radical changes. You must be determined that you will not turn back to your old ways or quit when things get tough. You have to see beyond the cross, just like Jesus, who, for the joy set before Him, endured the cross (see Heb. 12:2). We endure for the joy set before us—the victory, blessings, and glory released to us for obeying Him.

GLORY REVOLUTION

Our ministry is known for the "Glory of God" transforming people. We see Heaven's glory come down in our meetings, resulting in many healings, miracles, signs and wonders, salvations, and deliverances. But even with all that, I feel in my heart that God has much more in store for us as His children and that we're just barely scratching the surface of what His glory can really do in and to and through us. God told me that He wants His glory to invade not just our spirit, soul, and body, but even our personal lives. Yes, God wants to get "up close and personal" with us. He told me that, if His people would let His glory into their personal lives and their relationships, there will be not only a revival in this area among God's people, but also a "Glory Revolution."

God showed me prophetically that He is going to take it to the next level, from revival to revolution. Revival is not God's ultimate goal or the final destination for His people. Revival is only phase one of three phases. *Revival* is the awakening of God's people from slumber, the state of coming alive from a state of death. *Revolution* is the suite after revival. A revolution is a complete and forcible overthrow of an established government or political system, a radical pervasive change in society and the social structure, especially one made suddenly and often accompanied by violence.[1]

This means that the glory of God will invade and permeate God's children after they are radically revived from the dead, and it will bring them into the fire of their purpose and destiny. This will cause a sudden and abrupt revolution—a complete and radical overthrow of the present system and spiritual structure. It will be a spiritual revolution initiated by masses of God's people who are filled with and moving in God's glory and power. They will cast out demons in the name of Jesus, speak in tongues, heal the sick, and preach the Word of God everywhere.

All the while, the Lord will confirm their message through signs and miracles. This revolution will include all who are called His sons and daughters at any age level, but it will be spear-headed by the youth. Such is the picture that the Lord showed me of the kind of revolution that He intends to bring, which will spread all across America and to the nations. It will be contagious and unstoppable. This is phase two.

Phase three will be the *ruling and reigning of God's people* here on earth and continuing on to the new earth, where we will rule and reign not just over our situations, earthly troubles, and the forces of darkness, but even over the very elements of the earth, the animals, creation, time, and gravity, etc. When God's children walk in awesome consecration, holiness, glory, and power, we will rock this world like never before. There will be opposition, but we will see only their defeat because God is on our side. This is when no weapon that is formed against us will succeed due to the level of authority and power that we will be walking and operating in (see Isa. 54:15,17).

When God's people grab hold of this revelation concerning the mysteries and purpose of singleness in His glory, the result will revolutionize not only the singles in the Body of Christ, but also marriages and families. It will affect all relationships because before there were families, there were married couples. And before there were married couples, there were single individuals.

It is time for God's children to stand up and be forerunners of this new generation of people who are so consumed with the glory of God that every area of their life oozes the glory of Heaven. Then we shall see the complete fulfillment of Jesus' promise that *"the gates of hell shall not prevail against it [the church]"* (Matt, 16:18). Think of the kind of impact that we will have in this world and the world to come as more of us live our lives in complete surrender to God, observing His ways and ordinances without compromise or reservation, living our natural lives supernaturally and our supernatural lives naturally.

> *Behold! I have given you authority and power to trample upon serpents and scorpions, and [physical and mental strength and ability] over all the power that the enemy [possesses], and nothing shall in any way harm you* (Luke 10:19).

We have yet to see this verse fulfilled in every way in its fullness by the Church. But I believe that we are at the crest of it as we revolutionize how we live every area of our lives with the truth and power of God's Word as true sons and daughters of God. No more diluted versions of His truth and ways—we want it in concentrated form, including all of the vitamins and nutrition. Why wait until something is broken before we apply His truth and ways. The best way to avoid unnecessary suffering is to take proactive steps toward prevention.

ENDNOTE

1. *Microsoft Dictionary,* 2004, s.v. v. "Revival," "Revolution."

chapter 8

PREPARATION—AN OBLIGATION, NOT AN OPTION

*N*ow when the turn of each maiden came to go in to King Ahasuerus, after the regulations for the women had been carried out for twelve months, since this was the regular period for their beauty treatments, six months with oil and myrrh and six months with sweet spices and perfumes and the things for the purifying of the women (Esther 2:12).

The writer of the Book of Esther, who was inspired by the Holy Spirit, could easily have omitted the part about Esther's preparation and simply told us that she became queen, continuing with the rest of the story. But because the preparation time played a fundamental part in Esther's rise to the throne, God made sure that this crucial period was included in the story. It is crucial that we understand the importance of preparation and purification before we receive God's blessing or rise to the next level. A person can't get married without preparing for the necessary commitment and responsibility. Failure to prepare for marriage is like jumping into the deep waters without first learning how to swim. The result is catastrophic. A person preparing for marriage needs a clear understanding of the role that he or she is expected to play. Do your part and trust God to do His: *"Commit your way to the Lord [roll and repose each care of your load on Him]; trust (lean on, rely on and be confident) also in Him and He will bring it to pass"* (Ps. 37:5).

WHAT IS MARRIAGE MATERIAL?

Just like with Esther, how you prepare yourself for marriage will determine the quality of the marriage you'll get. Basically, *you get what you put into it.* If you don't want to end up as a divorce statistic or as part of a troubled marriage, then make preparing for it a priority.

To start, you need to know what marriage material looks like—you need to know what qualities need to be present in a person, indicating that they are well-prepared for marriage. A lot of people pick mates based on good looks, a sense of humor, how fun they are, or how nice they are. You need more than those things to make not just a successful marriage, but also a marriage that glorifies God and that exceeds what the world has ever seen or dreamed of. But in order to obtain that, we have to do our part.

The following areas are crucial components of a person who is good "marriage material":

1. Spiritually Strong

Marry a believer whose spiritual temperature is burning hot. For the woman, you want a man as hot as you or even hotter than you since the man is the head of the house. You want a mate who habitually knows, hears, and obeys God's voice and does His will. That way, when you marry, he will know how to lead his family at the center of His will. It is also good for the woman to already have a lifestyle of knowing, hearing, and obeying God's voice and will so that she won't be a hindrance to her husband when he wants to do what God tells him. Instead, she will confirm God's will and be one in spirit with her husband.

Marry someone who loves Jesus more than you, and not one who would love you more than God. Love for Jesus must be utmost. Your future spouse should exhibit continuing proof of spiritual growth, and so should you. If the person hasn't been actively involved in church before your relationship, don't expect it to be different after the wedding. *Whatever habits and ways a person has before you knew them will most likely be the same after you are married.*

There must be a common commitment to the Kingdom of God. Couples who do not share similar life goals are *not* right for each other. There must be common beliefs; otherwise there will be conflict, especially regarding raising children and leading the family. Even though you may have the same call or vision, it could still be a trap from the enemy. Make sure that God is the only One making the relationship happen. You can't go by logical similarities or even compatibility with one another; it still has to be supernaturally orchestrated by God.

2. Emotionally Secure

To be secure emotionally is to know who you are in Christ.

Marrying someone who is insecure makes you feel like you are walking on eggshells, afraid of saying or doing something that would cause them to explode or attack you. When people have major emotional problems, it means that they are struggling with unforgiveness and resentment and that they tend to have misplaced anger. Misplaced anger happens when they project their anger onto someone who did not cause their hurt. If they had an abusive past, had a lot of rejection, or didn't receive a lot of love and approbation from parents, and if they have not gone through deep inner healing and deliverance from those issues, then they are likely to react in fear, anger, and even violence to protect themselves.

People's unhealed emotions normally manifest in being easily offended, angered, snappy, controlling, and bitter and in struggling to forgive and love those who have hurt them, whether unintentionally or not. Other symptoms include being clingy, easily jealous, overly possessive, suspicious, or paranoid (which could result from experiences of abandonment or infidelity while growing up). If these manifestations are evident in people's lives, they are not ready for marriage or a relationship.

If you are contemplating marriage, it is best to deal with issues like this while you are still single. Let the cross of Christ have its complete work in you. When you are secure in Christ, nothing and no one offends you or moves you because you are deeply rooted and grounded in Him and His love. *The only thing that truly matters to you is what Jesus thinks of you, not anyone else.* That is what makes people secure emotionally and qualifies them for marriage.

3. Good Family Relations

Family relations do not have to be perfect, but if there is much strife, anger, bitterness, control, division, and discord, take these as warning signs. It's one thing if a person's family is not on good terms with that person due to their commitment to Jesus, but if it's because they themselves mistreat their own family, are selfish, arrogant, controlling, demeaning, mean or violent, then have nothing to do with that person. They will likely treat you in the same manner once you are married.

4. Decorum

Potential spouses need to display a level of decency concerning their appearance and behavior. If they are neglectful of their appearance (grooming and hygiene), it's usually a sign of neglect in other areas of their lives. There may be other issues underneath that neglect that need to be dealt with, like low self-esteem, rejection, rebellion, etc. On the other hand, much could be said about the other extreme—being too obsessed about how they look and dress. Some people are so consumed about looking perfect in every way outwardly that they refuse to let anyone see them undone. This is a major sign of insecurity and obsessiveness. Find a good balance—looking good outwardly in a healthy and decent way without being vain is the key.

5. Physical Wellbeing

If you want someone who is physically fit, strong, and healthy, you must fit into the same category too. Exercise is good and beneficial for everyone. It makes you sharper mentally, relieves stress, is great for circulation, eliminates toxins, and keeps you healthy, strong, toned, and fit. You have a much better overall feeling of health and wellness.

Eating healthy goes together with overall fitness. During this preparation time, purpose to free yourself from any addictions and vices that are harmful to your health. Start making changes to improve your quality of life while you are still single.

6. Self-control

Discern if the person you are considering marrying has self-control. Does your potential spouse practice self-control regarding sexual drive, passions, behavior, emotions, temper, spending, finances, and time? Does that person have a good sense of discipline and act responsibly? If there is an area in their life where they are off balance or lack self-control, then there are probably other areas in their life that are out of control. People should never take advantage of the one they are planning to marry in any way—sexually, emotionally, mentally, physically, financially, or spiritually.

> Run from anything that stimulates youthful lusts. Instead, pursue righteous living, faithfulness, love, and peace. Enjoy the companionship of those who call on the Lord with pure hearts (2 Timothy 2:22 NLT).

People who are in a godly and God-ordained relationship should earnestly guard each other's self-respect, purity, dignity, and well-being. If there is any compromise in any of those areas, that means trouble. If one causes the other to sin, especially sexually, then the spiritually stronger person must quickly end that relationship and not make excuses. Who is that person trying to please? Whatever problems they have in their pre-marital relationship will not be solved by marriage. They will only bring them into their marriage. Research reveals that men and women who have sex before marriage are much more likely to be sexually unfaithful to their spouse during marriage than those who do not.[1] Once the pattern is established, it is extremely difficult to break it.

There are also those with bad and out-of-control tempers. If a person loses their temper with their parents and siblings or with anyone that doesn't let them have their way, that person will do the same with you. If they managed to conceal it from you during your pre-marital relationship, then they will let it all out once you are married. People whose childhood situations were like a war-zone are likely to turn their marriages into the same. Generally a man will treat his wife the way he treats his mother, and a woman will respond to her husband the way she responds to her father.

7. Good Credit Score

It is well-known that financial problems cause marital distress and divorce.[2] Yet many marry with little to no thought of how to handle finances correctly. If you can barely support yourself in your current financial situation, then you are not ready to marry. If your potential spouse has a bad credit score, it is a strong indication that they are irresponsible with their finances. If they have accumulated a lot of debt, that means that they lack spending self-control. If they are that way before you marry, they'll have that same habit of spending afterward. *Make sure they have self-control and discipline and are wise and good stewards of their finances.*

HONEST SELF-EVALUATION

Whether or not you are currently in a relationship, take a few minutes now to consider honestly your answers to the following questions:

- Would a relationship with the opposite sex right now be best for me?

- Is this what God wants in my life right now? What about for the one I'm dating?

- What have I done and pursued that has truly prepared me in every way to form a godly and pure relationship that could lead to a godly marriage?

- Can I truly say that, based on where I am at the present time spiritually, emotionally, mentally, vocationally, and financially, I am totally ready for marriage?

- Am I able to provide for a wife and family at this point of my life? Am I ready to be a godly leader and loving husband?

- Am I ready to be a godly and submissive wife?

- Have I established a close enough relationship with my church leaders? Can they speak freely into my life and teach, instruct, and guide me in all of the affairs of my life? Can I freely discuss with and submit to them any interest or plans that I have concerning my future? Or have I been doing things on my own, and am submitted to no one but myself?

BECOME THAT PERSON

Another thing that must be emphasized is the importance of becoming the kind of person that you want to marry. Be for the other person what you want them to be for you. If you are believing for someone who is physically fit and who works out, then you need to make sure that you are in shape as well. If you are believing for someone who is on fire for God, spiritually mature, and walking in obedience, then make sure that you are not lukewarm and spiritually shallow. If you are believing for someone who has godly character, integrity, and purity, then you had better be a person of equally high standards. Become like the person you are believing for.

That's exactly what I did, and that's exactly what I got. I worked out regularly and got physically fit, and so did my husband before I met him. I kept myself hot for God, and so did David. I obeyed God in all that He asked me to do, and David did the same. I was a chaste virgin, and so was he. We matched each other perfectly. I didn't settle for second best. I *waited* for God's best, and *He gave him to me.* I let Him do the choosing and the giving; I just waited and believed.

READY OR NOT?

Marriage is a serious commitment. It's more than just a union of two separate souls, coming together to combine their pasts and create a future. Imagine, you are actually giving yourself wholly to another person—and that includes everything about you—all of your past and present. Are you willing and ready to be totally vulnerable in all senses of the word to this other person, withholding nothing, keeping no secrets? Are you ready to deal with all of the baggage that this person is bringing into your life? You are investing your whole life, hoping that you will reap the reward of a lifelong partner who will always stay by your side, both through the good times and the bad. But how sure are you that it will happen just like that, that it won't end in divorce (which is growing rampant today)? What kind of preparations have you done beforehand to equip you in order to build a lasting, godly marriage that has God's purposes in mind and not your own?

Lovesick couples need to take the time to truly contemplate the ramifications of the decision that they are about to make before God. Can they separate themselves from the emotional and sexual urges that intoxicate them and sensibly determine if this union is truly from God and if they are ready to make this lifetime investment? Do they really know the person they are about to be bound to? Do they truly know themselves?

Too often, the wonderful and exciting aspects of the wedding ceremony and its splendor surpass the magnitude of the commitment. The worry is more about who to invite, who's doing what, and who's saying what rather than the reality of marriage. Can they say with complete confidence that God truly put them together? Are they really ready to walk together down the aisle of uncertainty?

How Does a Man Prepare for Marriage?

The following is a list for men to consider:

1. Leadership Role

"But I want you to know and realize that Christ is the Head of every man, the head of a woman is her husband, and the Head of Christ is God" (1 Cor. 11:3). In this Scripture, Paul is showing us that the chain of headship starts with God the Father as the Head of Christ, then flows down to Christ as the Head of the man (husband), and finally to the husband as the head of the woman (wife). Here is a biblically accurate picture of the role of the husband, who will eventually take on the role of a father. He is to represent Christ to his wife and children. That is an awesome responsibility, and a sacred privilege!

In today's society, I have observed that more and more men are not taking their leadership roles in the family and are instead becoming passive and indecisive. They normally pair themselves up with strong women who take charge. That is not how God designed men and women to interact. Now I do believe in women in ministry and in women holding leadership roles when it comes to ministry and their jobs, but when it comes to marriage, the man is called to be the head leader. He leads and makes the ultimate decisions. The wife can equally share what she feels from God, her opinion, or her advice, but the husband is to make the final decision, especially when it comes to the major ones. She can make decisions in areas where her husband is weak or has no interest, but she is not to take control and manipulate him or demean him in any way.

On the other hand, there are also men who are abusive and overly controlling. The wife basically becomes a doormat and is not valued or revered as an equal partner. She can't say or do anything unless her husband allows her. These husbands become dictators and operate in a "macho" spirit, making their wives their slaves in unwholesome and unreciprocated submission, lacking immensely in their ability to appropriately love and value them.

In this case, the husbands are mistreating their wives and are not obeying their biblical role as it is written:

Out of respect for Christ, be courteously reverent to one another. Wives, understand and support your husbands in ways that show your support for Christ. The husband provides leadership to his wife the way Christ does to His Church, not by domineering but by cherishing. So just as the Church submits to Christ as He exercises such leadership, wives should likewise submit to their husbands.

Husbands, go all out in your love for your wives, exactly as Christ did for the Church—a love marked by giving, not getting. Christ's love makes the Church whole. His words evoke her beauty. Everything He does and says is designed to bring the best out of her, dressing her in dazzling white silk, radiant with holiness. And that is how husbands ought to love their wives. They're really doing themselves a favor—since they're already "one" in marriage. No one abuses his own body, does he? No, he feeds and pampers it. That's how Christ treats us, the Church, since we are part of His body.

And this is why a man leaves father and mother and cherishes his wife. No longer two, they become "one flesh." This is a huge mystery, and I don't pretend to understand it all. What is clearest to me is the way Christ treats the Church. And this provides a good picture of how each husband is to treat his wife, loving himself in loving her, and how each wife is to honor her husband (Ephesians 5:21-33 TM).

That Scripture clearly explains the appropriate roles for the husband and wife and how each should treat the other. While being the head, taking on the leading role to the wife, the husband is to love and cherish her. Men were created as initiators while women were created to respond. Basically, if a husband is not happy with how his wife is treating him, it is good to check what kind of treatment he is giving her; she responds to the treatment that she is being given. Men need to learn and develop how to cherish their wives and how to love them with words, gestures, and actions. The wife will respond with respect and honor to her husband and be supportive of him as she feels secure and cherished by him.

Husbands, if you complain that your wife dominates you, maybe it's because you give her too much power and liberty, more than she is suppose to have—to the point that you no longer have any say and can't make the most important decisions in the house. It is time for you to find your place and to put your foot down when you need to. Wives who naturally have stronger characters than their husbands need to practice yielding and learn to step back and help their man develop his take-charge attitude. Wives need to help their husbands gain confidence in decision-making, leading, and making good judgments. Wives must be gracious enough to make room for mistakes. They can still be themselves, but more submitted, respectful, honoring, and supportive to their husbands' leadership role.

Men, get your example from the Bible, from Jesus—how He loves, cherishes, and sacrificed for the Church, His Bride. He is the greatest and the most romantic Lover of all. Learn how He leads, loves, and relates to His Bride. Lead by knowing how to hear God's voice and promptings. Be sensitive to the leading of the Holy Spirit. Have eyes to see and ears to hear. Know God's Word so that you will know when God is speaking and not the devil. God will never make you do something against His Word. Lead by example and not by word only, not with a whip, but through godly conduct and behavior. Serve others well before you expect others to serve you. Give respect to others before expecting them to respect you.

2. Godly Character

"Their purpose [the Proverbs] is to teach people wisdom and discipline, to help them understand the insights of the wise. Their purpose is to teach people to live disciplined and successful lives, to help them do what is right, just, and fair" (Prov. 1:2-3 NLT).

Every man needs to develop godly character. Learn from God's Word how to be the man God created you to be. When I was a teenager, I made it a habit to read and meditate on a chapter of Proverbs a day. It helped me become wise and discerning and to make good judgments. There are 31 chapters, a whole month's worth. Read a chapter for each day of the month. Then you can read it 12 times a year. You can never get enough wisdom (see Prov. 4:5-15; 24:5-6).

Develop these character traits before you contemplate marriage; apply as you desire to be whole in your singleness:

- **Humility.** Be humble yet confident in who you are in Christ and not in yourself alone, not too proud to admit when you are wrong, able to accept the blame and apologize when the fault is yours. Learn to receive constructive criticism and correction when needed. Be humble enough to hear someone out and let them be right from time to time. *"...Humility comes before honor. Humility and the fear of the Lord bring wealth and honor and life"* (Prov. 15:33b; 22:4 NIV).

- **Integrity.** Have integrity in word and deed. Keep your word. Be honest in your dealings with yourself and others. Put away every falsehood and pretense from your words and actions. *"The man of integrity walks securely, but he who takes crooked paths will be found out"* (Prov. 10:9 NIV) *"The Lord detests lying lips, but He delights in men who are truthful"* (Prov. 12:22 NIV).

- **Wisdom.** Be a man of wisdom and not foolishness, knowing how to make good and wise judgments according to God's standards, not just logical ones. Have discernment. Consider well your words, steps, and actions. *"How much better to get wisdom than gold, and good judgment than silver To acquire wisdom is to love oneself; people who cherish understanding will prosper"* (Prov. 16:16; 19:8 NLT).

- **Purity.** Be pure in your motives and intentions. Treat woman as you would your own mother and sister—with respect, dignity, and pure and holy love, not with lust, indecency, anger, aggression, or violence. *"Don't let anyone think less of you because you are young. Be an example to all believers in what you say, in the way you live, in your love, your faith, and your purity"* (1 Tim. 4:12 NLT).

- **Self-control.** Control your passions, desires, temper spending, eating, even work—don't be a workaholic. *"...Supplement your faith with a generous provision of moral excellence, and moral excellence with knowledge, and knowledge with self-control, and self-control with patient endurance, and patient endurance with godliness,"* (2 Peter 1:5-6 NLT).

- **Peace.** Learn to be at peace with yourself and others. Do not stir up strife and get into heated arguments. Learn to settle matters in a peaceful and gentle way. *"Look at those who are honest and good, for a wonderful future awaits those who love peace"* (Ps. 37:37 NLT).

- **Humor.** Be a man with a good sense of humor. Learn to laugh at your enemies, when things are not going well, at your own mistakes, weaknesses, and imperfections. Lighten up and have fun. Don't take yourself too seriously. Every woman appreciates a good laugh, as long as it is not demeaning someone else. *"...for the joy of the Lord is your* *strength and stronghold* (Neh. 8:10b).

- **Manners.** It is never too late to learn how to be a gentleman. When you lead with good manners, a woman will respond in like manner. Be courteous, polite, grateful, considerate, and thoughtful. No woman can resist a well-mannered man.

- **Romance.** Learn from the Song of Solomon how our God is a romantic kind of lover. Learn how to genuinely love and cherish the woman God has chosen to be your wife. It is worth the time and the effort as you will not regret her response. *"Husbands, go all out in your love for your wives, exactly as Christ did for the church—a love marked by giving, not getting. Christ's love makes the church whole. His words evoke her beauty. Everything he does and says is designed to bring out the best out of her...And that is how husbands ought to love their wives..."* (Eph. 5:25-27 TM).

- **Gentleness.** Be kind and gentle when giving correction. Be thoughtful and considerate, especially with chores and in speech. *"Kind words heal and help; cutting words wound and maim* (Prov. 15:4 TM).

- **Fear of the Lord.** The beginning of wisdom is the fear of the Lord. Fear and please God, not others. Care more about what God thinks than what others may think. Have the mind of Christ—a godly perspective. *"Fear of the Lord teaches wisdom..."* (Prov. 15:33 NLT).

- **Optimism**. Always think and bring out the best in others. Be positive in your conduct and speech. Be an encourager. Be quick to give compliments and slow to anger and criticize.

- **Diligence.** Be hardworking and diligent and you will receive your just reward and live in plenty, not in want. Be a good provider. If you are diligent, God will bless and prosper whatever your hands shall do. Lazy people never succeed in life and will always crave and dream for things, but never obtain them. No woman wants to marry someone who is lazy and irresponsible. *"Lazy hands make a man poor, but diligent hands bring wealth. The sluggard craves and gets nothing, but the desires of the diligent are fully satisfied"* (Prov. 10:4, 13:4 NIV).

- **Service**. Be someone who loves to serve others. As a single man, adopt a family with whom you can be a part of and find ways to serve and help. The best way you can prepare and train for marriage and a family is by serving one. You get to see the real work involved in making marriage work, and what it takes to be a great husband and father. This will also take away any false expectations in marriage that many have.

You can also serve in your local church, and other ministries that are doing good works for the Kingdom of God. You can serve by being a catcher, an usher, a driver, an intercessor, setting up equipment, cleaning, etc. You can also go on short-term missions and be a blessing to other nations. Live to give. Give of yourself in holy service and God will richly reward you. When you make your life a blessing to others, it will always come back to you. Serving others also keeps your mind off thoughts of loneliness as you surround yourself with God's family.

HOW DOES A WOMAN PREPARE FOR MARRIAGE?

I believe that women can learn a lot and benefit from the wisdom found in Proverbs as well. Develop the same godly characteristics as those listed for men, as well as the following additional characteristics that are vital for women:

- **Submission.** *"Wives, understand and support your husbands in ways that show your support for Christ. So just as the church submits to Christ as He exercises such leadership, wives should likewise submit to their husbands"* (Eph. 5:22,24 TM).

Paul is telling women how to be submissive, respectful, and supportive of their husbands. Treat your husband as you would Christ—honoring him and his leadership. In today's world, there are two extremes that we see among women: one kowtows like a doormat and the other dominates. Neither is good.

The doormat type allows herself to be mistreated, taken advantage of, and manipulated by her husband. She must learn when to say no, which is when he crosses the line of what is biblically appropriate and sound. On the contrary, the dominant type mistreats and manipulates her husband and likes to take charge. These women like to think, *Sure, the man is the head of the house, but the women are the neck that controls the head.* This type of woman must let her husband take charge and make the final decisions—giving him room to make mistakes. She may be her own boss at work or the leader of her organization, but when it comes to her home, she must allow her husband to be the head, and she must submit to and honor his leadership role.

Being submissive is not a sign of weakness. An honorable woman knows how to give honor and respect to others. *"...Christ is the Head of every man, the head of a woman is her husband, and the Head of Christ is God"* (1 Cor. 11:3). God wants us to know the order of things and to live accordingly. In His order, the husband is the head or leader of the wife, whether he has a strong, take charge character or not. This is what pleases God.

- **Discretion.** Women are strongly commended to be discreet—to be tactful, prudent, and cautious. Having discretion is often paired with having godly wisdom.

A woman who is beautiful but lacks discretion is like a gold ring in a pig's snout. My child, don't lose sight of common sense and discernment. Hang on to them, for they will refresh your soul. They are like jewels on a necklace. They keep you safe on your way, and your feet will not stumble. You can go to bed without fear; you will lie down and sleep soundly (Proverbs 11:22; 3:21-24 NLT).

Discretion means having the good judgment and sensitivity needed to avoid embarrassing or upsetting others, having the freedom or authority to judge something or make a decision about it, and having the ability to keep sensitive information secret. As women, we must learn to develop discretion. It can save us from a lot of trouble and helps us walk securely and confidently.

- **Gentleness**. We need to be gentle in our conduct and speech. When we operate in gentleness, it will soften hard hearts. When speaking our opinion, giving suggestions, constructive criticism, or correction, we should do it in gentleness of spirit—it will be better received than advice given in a harsh tone. *"A gentle answer turns away wrath, but a harsh word stirs up anger"* (Prov. 15:1 NIV).

- **Wisdom.** Be wise and make good judgments. Do not be foolish. Look and plan ahead. Listen to wise counsel. *"The foolish woman is noisy; she is simple and open to all forms of evil, she [willfully and recklessly] knows nothing whatever [of eternal value]. House and riches are the inheritance from fathers, but a wise, understanding, and prudent wife is from the Lord"* (Prov. 9:13; 19:14).

- **Peace**. Do not be quarrelsome, and do not nag. The Bible warns men to avoid such women. *"A foolish child is a calamity to a father; a quarrelsome wife is as annoying as constant dripping. It's better to live alone in the corner of an attic than with a quarrelsome wife in a lovely home"* (Prov. 19:13; 21:9 NLT).

- **Nobleness.**

"A wife of noble character is her husband's crown, but a disgraceful wife is like decay in his bones (Proverbs 12:4 NIV).

- **Modesty.**

What matters is not your outer appearance—the styling of your hair, the jewelry you wear, the cut of your clothes—but your inner disposition. Cultivate inner beauty, the gentle, gracious kind that God delights in. The holy women of old were beautiful before God that way, and were good, loyal wives to their husbands. Sarah, for instance, taking care of Abraham, would address his as "my dear husband." You'll be true daughters of Sarah if you do the same, unanxious and unintimidated (1 Peter 3:3-6 TM).

This is how women ought to be in God's design. A godly woman, abiding in the Holy Spirit, knows that it is not her outward appearance and adornment that is important, but her inner beauty and character. As she cultivates her inner beauty, gentleness, and graciousness—God takes pleasure in her. Out of that comes real beauty. You will be like the women of old, who treated their husbands with love and respect. When you become such a woman, you are indeed considered one of Sarah's daughters—not fearful or anxious, but trusting completely in God.

- **Domestic Skill.** Women need to know how to cook and clean. Many women today are oblivious when it comes to taking care of the home. They order out, and their homes are a mess. If you're one of those women, grab a cookbook and learn how to make a meal. If you want to have a happ husband—learn how to cook and how to make good, healthy foods. Learn a variety of dishes and specialties from different countries. Learn to bake so that, when you have children, they can enjoy eating Mama's cookies and desserts.

Learn how to clean the house. No one wants to live in a messy, dirty house. You will be the one to set the standard of cleanliness in your home. As they say, "Cleanliness is next to godliness." You will feel better about yourself when you are well able to do those things. Let's face it; your mom will not be living with you; so start learning now. Practice cooking and cleaning at home and try to bless other families with your abilities.

How You See Yourself Determines Who You Marry

"So you are complete through your union with Christ..." (Col. 2:10 NLT).

If you don't allow God to be your Matchmaker, how you see yourself will determine who you marry. If you have low self-esteem and don't have a positive and healthy regard for yourself, you will settle for anyone who shows any interest in you. But that kind of thinking is dangerous and can get you into trouble. God is the King of kings, and we are His royal children. As God's royal children, we're not just any kids on the block. God treats us differently than He treats those who are not His. He has great plans and promises for us, and He picks the best for His Kingdom.

We need to start seeing ourselves as children of a King with very high standards, not as orphans who are starving for love and affection from anybody. Orphans have low standards because they have never felt a sense of belonging. But we belong to the richest and most honorable family—God's family. So we must keep our standards high and never compromise them for anyone. Rather than doing the choosing for ourselves, we must be content to let our heavenly Father choose and arrange for us.

THE PARENTS' RESPONSIBILITY

Parents have a significant responsibility above all else to see that their children become whole and complete in God as singles and to prepare them to fulfill God's call and purposes in their lives. Young people are naturally full of energy and passion. They are looking for a cause to be passionate about, something to give their love, devotion, service, and even their lives to. Deep inside, children are crying out, Isn't there a cause? *Isn't there something in this life that is bigger than what I can see and understand, yet that I can somehow be a part of? What is my purpose here on earth?*

This is a crucial time in their lives, a time of great personal growth and development, and parents can help them find answers by being there for them, encouraging them, and giving them godly (not worldly) wisdom and guidance. In addition, parents can involve them in ministries that will be highly beneficial for their call and gifts. Youth need parents to direct their energy and passion toward God and His Kingdom, to help them find their place and destiny in Him, and to help keep their focus only on Him.

But instead of equipping them with the character, education, and experience necessary to fulfill God's purposes in their lives, many parents allow their children be distracted by dating. Parents must keep all forms of distraction, even those that might seem good and harmless in the natural, away from their children. Parents need to take a stand for their children and say, *Distractions—Get out and stay out!*

One way to achieve this goal is by *praying for each child's future and destiny in God.* Whether marriage is part of their futures or not, praying for God's will for their lives and covering in prayer the chosen mates God has for them is the best thing that parents can do—beginning when they are born. Parents need not wait to start praying for their children's destinies and future mates until they are teens or high school graduates.

If you are a parent and want your children to seek God's best in life and marriage, show them that it's working for you. Let your life and marriage set the standard; be the kind of parent that they would desire to be. It hurts children when they see their parents rebelling against God, living in compromise and hypocrisy, or fighting and mistreating one another. But when there is peace, joy, love, harmony, respect, and most of all, the fear of God and God-consciousness in a home, it makes them feel secure. *You must teach by example.* Show and teach them selfless and unconditional love, holiness, self-control, respect, obedience, and sacrifice to God as you demonstrate to them these virtues through your life. That's how they learn.

It's also crucial that you teach them to submit to God's way of establishing relationships—to wait for God's best and to trust Him as the only one who knows the perfect who, when, and how. You must take time to instill these truths into your children in your everyday life—while cooking, cleaning the car, going shopping, or playing ball, especially concerning marriage. It's imperative that you explain biblically how God designed marriage until they have understanding of His divine plan. That way, when they begin to contemplate marriage, they will want to pattern their lives and goals after God's divine design. As they get older, they will need your godly advice and guidance in making the right decisions. *It's worth investing your time now, as they don't stay young forever.* You'll be thanking yourself later when you see them married to the ones God has chosen for them, with a blessed and successful marriage.

When it comes to young people and their raging hormones, entrusting them with too much dating liberty is unwise and dangerous, especially when they're allowed to go out alone. That is why it is best to abandon dating as a whole. Teach them the many dangerous consequences of dating. As parents, it's easy to blame your children for being rebellious and to be frustrated with the foolish decisions that they make. That way you don't have to feel responsible. But the truth is, you're to blame for not taking the time to teach your children and to explain to them that dating is wrong and that God has a better use for their energy and passion in His Kingdom that won't compromise their purity and standards. You're responsible for instructing them and for keeping them from doing the wrong things and hurting themselves and others in the process.

If you've made mistakes in life concerning relationships and marriage, then you have all the more reason to warn and educate your children. If you're ignorant about things that pertain to healthy and godly relationships, then *educate yourself* and find the proper materials and teachings. Take the time to help, instruct, and guide your children into God's ways.

When your children become adolescents, you should change your training approach. When the right foundation has been laid in their earlier years, it's easier to guide them when they are older. If that's not the case in your home, it's better to start now. Ask God for His strength, grace, and wisdom to help you uphold His standards in the face of the intense pressure that your children feel to accept less than God's best for them. You may seek assistance from your pastors concerning your children, but the overall responsibility lies with *you*.

Don't just be a "friend" regarding dating and relationships. What teens really need is a loving parent to teach and guide them to do the right things. By forfeiting your authority as their parent in order to be their "friend" (a confidant with no authority), you lose them as your children, thus defying your main duty and obligation—representing God to them and practicing your God-given authority. Parents do their children a disservice by creating a false image of God and His authority and by molding them without a sense of security, stability, and responsibility.

Note: if you are single and your parent(s) are unbelievers, find a spiritually strong, mature, wise, and discerning couple to guide you, counsel you, equip you, and hold you accountable. Don't make the mistake of raising yourself in the relationship journey. In addition to seeking Christian adults, read books and other teaching materials concerning godly relationships before you attempt to be in one.

Don't develop a bad habit of dating and then wonder why things aren't working out the way that you expected or that you saw in a movie. Learn from the truth and only from the truth, which is the Word of God.

ENDNOTES

1. www.thecoolchurch.com.

2. "Divorce Prevention: Causes of Divorce and How We Can Prevent Divorce," *Oklahoma Marriage Initiative,* http://www.okmarriage.org/Services/DivorcePrevention.asp (accessed 12 September 2008).

GOD IS YOUR MATCHMAKER

THE HISTORY OF MARRIAGE

"Then the Lord God made a woman from the rib, and He brought her to the man" (Gen. 2:22 NLT). From Genesis to Revelation, from the first act in Eden to the last act in the heavens, the central theme of human history is marriage. Throughout this unfolding drama, God Himself isn't merely a remote spectator. He initiates the action and brings it to its climax. From beginning to end, He is totally and personally involved in marriage.

First, the concept of marriage originated entirely with God. Adam had no part in it. He wasn't in need of anyone, nor was he so depressed from being alone that he had to manipulate God to give him a mate. It was God, not Adam, who decided that he needed a wife. He was fully satisfied in life and in his relationship with God.

Second, it was God who formed Eve for Adam. He alone knew the kind of mate that Adam needed. Third, it was God who presented Eve to Adam. Adam didn't have to go looking for her. And fourth, it was God who determined the way in which Adam and Eve were to relate to each other. The end purpose of their relationship was perfect unity: *"Therefore a man shall leave his father and mother and be joined to his wife, and they shall become one flesh"* (Gen. 2:24 NKJV).

If God's pattern for marriage remains unchanged for Christians today, then the four truths outlined above still apply in our lives. In practical terms, what does this mean? Primarily it means that Christians will enter into marriage not because it is their decision, but because it is God's. He has not left something as serious as marriage for us to figure out on our own without any instructions and principles to go by. It doesn't work that way.

I believe God can speak clearly to us concerning marriage and how to go about it His way. As Christians, we are a people who, although living in this world, are not of this world (see Rom. 12:2; 2 Cor. 6:14-18). We are children of the Most High God and citizens of Heaven. We should adapt our way of living to what is biblical and has eternal value. We are a people who are set apart for His purposes and not for ours. The main emphasis here is *His* purposes.

Think about it. To get a driver's license requires instruction and training. So why is there very little to no instruction or training regarding relationships and marriage? What requirements must be met before a couple is granted a marriage license? A driver's license at least requires a test to demonstrate some level of knowledge, experience, and competency with a motor vehicle before one is turned loose on the highway. Yet many churches today are willing to turn a couple loose with each other's lives for a "love gift" and a signature at the courthouse.

The only lessons about marriage that most married people received came from watching their parents (who also learned from their parents), television, and movies. With each generation, the state of marriage gets worse and worse as our society continues to degenerate and delegate. Fewer family values are upheld today than 40 years ago. Hollywood couldn't care less if your life doesn't end "happily ever after."

We went to school to learn how to read and write, how to add and subtract. But rarely are there classes or seminars in church that teach people how to prepare for marriage and how to understand their responsibilities and roles according to God's plan. Too many were never taught what to expect in a relationship, how to behave in one, how to relate to the opposite sex in a godly way (without compromising their standards), how to wait for God's best and not settle for anyone less, how to be a godly husband or wife, and especially what to do to save your marriage if it starts to fall apart.

As a result, many Christians end up choosing their mates for the wrong reasons and then proceed into marriage with ill-defined skills, goals, and expectations. This is one reason for the large number of dysfunctional families. Chances are, if your parents were from dysfunctional families, then their parents probably were too. You must choose to change things in your life in order to stop the ugly cycle. Only the blood of Jesus can break those things off of you and bring forgiveness and restoration.

We need to unlearn and eliminate all of the dysfunctional ideas that have been passed on to us. It is time to re-educate ourselves the right way—from God's Manual, learning His ways concerning healthy and godly relationships and truly seeking out people and materials that will help us achieve and maintain them. It won't happen, though, unless there is effort on your part.

God offers that which represents Christ accurately to a lost world. He offers marriage with destiny and purpose, partnering together for dominion (see Gen. 1:28), to produce godly seed (see Mal. 2:15), and to portray Christ's relationship with His Bride, the Church (see Eph. 5:23-33).

ARRANGED MARRIAGES

Long ago, arranged marriages were fully accepted as part of the culture in many countries. Some countries and cultures still have this practice today. In fact, I know a strong Christian girl whose parents came from India but now live in the United States. Her parents arranged whom she should marry—and it worked out well. They are happily married to this day and have three children.

Another modern-day example is found in the Jewish Orthodox community, which still practices arranged marriages. In every village, there is a matchmaker (*shad khan* in Hebrew) who matches a couple in everything from the degree of their spirituality to their looks, personalities, and social status. The perfect match would have as many similarities as possible, yet retain enough differences so that they complement each other.

The *shad khan* is very well paid and possesses outstanding credibility. Initially the couple is allowed to meet in a public setting and have a simple conversation without any touching or other physical contact. The public setting keeps the encounter pure and blameless. If there is chemistry between them, then they proceed with the wedding. The parents are totally involved from the very beginning.

To this day, dating is not allowed in this religious Jewish culture. The only "date," if it can be called that, is that one-time meeting in the public setting for conversation. Some parents even consider that meeting to be risky and troublesome enough, so many couples don't see each other at all until after they are pronounced husband and wife. The purpose of this extreme caution is to minimize the chances of arousing lust.

These arranged marriages in the orthodox community have an impressive track record for longevity. By and large, very few end in divorce. Generally they are happy and wholesome families where the children are very submissive to their parents. Conservative religious Jews date and even hold hands, but nothing more than that. Secular Jews have similar practices to modern-day non-believers.

In Bible days, it was normally the father who served as the *shad khan* and arranged marriages for his children. If for any reason he was unable to do this task, he delegated it to a trustee such as what may have happened in Genesis 15 with Abraham and Eliezer. In this pattern, the boy's father decided and arranged the marriage with the girl's father, and it was done without the children's input. The children had to accept their parents' decision and trust that they knew what was best for them. The marriage would take place before the two even have a chance to truly get to know each other. Love was something that was learned after they were married. Theoretically, that's where it really gets exciting and romance begins! Since they have a lifetime to get to know each other and develop love, it is no wonder that the romance and passion can last unto death. Unfortunately, however, there are some arranged marriages where abuse and violence exist, such as in some Middle Eastern and Muslim cultures where this type of male-domination behavior is accepted.

COURTSHIP AND DATING

Neither courtship nor dating came from the Bible. They are practices the world invented. Dating really is what evolved from courtship (as discussed in Chapter 2). Similar to dating, some courtships result in marriage, while others result in the couple simply remaining friends.

What does God's Word say? With God as our Matchmaker, our *shad khan,* there are no loose ends, no faulty system, no tricks, no fleshly operations—it's all God. God is still very much into arranged marriages, and He is the One who arranges them. He's the Matchmaker, the *shad khan* of His children. This eliminates the need for any human effort, as well as the need for people to try and impress each other. It's all God, and it's all good! He doesn't need our help to make it happen.

Abraham did not depend on his human wisdom or criteria in choosing a wife for Isaac. He did not depend on human wisdom and did not judge according to appearance or social standards, but he relied fully on God's guidance. God was always involved, from beginning to end. Isaac didn't meet Rebekah until she was presented to him to be his bride. He knew that God and his father Abraham would find his perfect match.

God also brought Ruth and Boaz together supernaturally (see Ruth 2-4). As Ruth devoted her life to taking care of her widowed mother-in-law, Naomi, God rewarded her with a husband from Naomi's family. She wasn't asking or looking for a husband. She was complete in her singleness and was diligently caring for Naomi. Again, God used and guided the parent, in this case, Naomi, to choose and arrange the marriage for Ruth. She was the one who advised Ruth to go to Boaz's field to gather wheat and then to lie on Boaz's threshing floor etc, which ultimately led to their marriage. God knew who and when for Ruth's marriage. This union was of great importance because they were part of the lineage of Jesus. Imagine that! Certainly there was no accident or happenstance there.

God didn't arrange marriages only in the Old Testament. How about the union of Mary and Joseph (see Matt. 1-2; Luke 1)? God even used angels to speak to each of them throughout their betrothal, even after Jesus' birth, as they escaped to Egypt. You can't get more supernatural than that. God arranged their union; in fact, He orchestrated every part of Jesus' genealogy. The fact that the first chapter of the Book of Matthew lists all of their names shows that God had divinely chosen Mary and Joseph to be Jesus' earthly parents, even generations before they were born.

God is still sitting on His throne, aware of everything and everyone. Nothing escapes Him. To all who will listen, He makes His will crystal clear. There are no gray areas with God. Everything is black and white. That's how God speaks and operates. God is not fickle like we are. Whatever God says is not open for modification. His ways are very different from ours (see Isa. 55:8-9 NLT).

Since God is our Father and is always speaking to us about all of the major issues of life, why would He be silent or unconcerned when it comes to telling His children who they should marry? Why would He stop being our Lord and take the back seat when it comes to choosing our marriage partners? God would not neglect such an important event in our lives. If we let God choose for us, the outcome will always be favorable.

It is high time for singles to want something better in relationships. But things won't improve unless people are desperate enough to want to change! Someone defined insanity as *doing the same things over and over again but expecting a different result.* We have to change our values, mindsets, belief-systems, priorities, and attitudes. The question is, how badly do we want a better life in God and in our relationships?

People are not love experts; God is. He is Love! Only He knows the innermost details about us. He alone qualifies as the One who can put two people together for a perfect match. Who are we, with our limited knowledge and capabilities, to try to take His rightful place in choosing who the right person is for us? We simply don't qualify for that responsibility.

The following is a simple diagram taken from a church manual on courtship written by pastors Dennis and Linda Trout. It illustrates the differences between worldly relationships and godly relationships:[1]

	Worldly Relationships	**Godly Relationship**
Friendship	Peer-Oriented	Family-Oriented
Dating/Courtship	For Pleasure	For Marriage
Engagement	Breakable Proposal	Binding Promise
Wedding Vows	Until Divorce	Till Death Do Us Part

STEPS TO A GODLY MARRIAGE

God is a covenant-making God. He made a lasting covenant with Israel, His chosen people, and with the Church. He made relationships to last, not to be discarded or changed frequently like clothing. Godly relationships involve commitment. The following are steps to a godly marriage:

1. Make a Commitment

When God presents you to the one He has chosen for you and confirms it in many legitimate ways, you should make a commitment to each other. As a genuine friendship through a healthy social bonding takes place, it is fine to take your relationship to the next level. But do discuss the relationship with both of your parents or spiritual parents (an accountability couple).

2. Find an Accountability Couple

The ideal people accountability couple is your parents, assuming that they are strong and mature Christians who will provide you with the prayers, guidance, direction, discernment, correction, and protection that you need as you submit your relationship to them. Hopefully one of the main sources of confirmation that you received concerning God's choice of that specific person as your mate came from them (ideally from their prayer, fasting, and honest seeking for and discerning of God's will for your life).

It is also good to have spiritual leaders, such as your pastors and others in full-time ministry, who you are connected with and who know you personally and can speak into your life. Make sure these people don't just approve of and marry every couple that desires to be together. If they have never refused to marry someone, that means that they don't bother to hear from God concerning each couple that comes to them. It also means that they are not suitable accountability people for you since they do not have God's standards concerning marriage and relationships. It is important to have the right leaders to speak God's truth over you—leaders who have godly wisdom and discernment and who make godly judgments rather than giving humanistic and natural counsel.

Proceed in the relationship only when there are genuine confirmations.

3. Cultivate Spiritual Bonding

Once the relationship has been tested, confirmed, and approved by parents and spiritual leaders, spiritual bonding can take place between the couple—the sharing of deep spiritual thoughts, beliefs, dreams, prophecies, and so forth.

4. Cultivate Emotional Bonding

As the relationship deepens, gradual emotional bonding can proceed as each person shares things concerning their lives, including their past, family life, and childhood. Romance can come into play in the form of giving of gifts and a limited amount of affection.

5. Cultivate Physical Bonding

On the wedding night, the couple experiences all of the physical bonding that they have long awaited. This is where the bonding of their physical bodies takes place—the marriage bed. A lifetime of love and romance awaits them.

6. Encourage Others to Do the Same

Spread this biblical teaching about the godly process toward a godly marriage to others.

ENDNOTE

1. Dennis and Linda Trout, *Against the Grain.*

chapter 10

MR. COUNTERFAKE VS. MR. RIGHT

God promised Abraham and his wife, Sarah, a son, but because they were of advanced age, Sarah tried to make it happen her way. Sarah offered her maidservant to her husband as a way to produce the promised child (see Gen. 16). When God promises something, He is well able to accomplish it. He doesn't need our help. Some think that, because He's taking too long (as if we know the right timing better than God), they need to give God a hand.

When we get involved, we seize control from God and usually end up with a mess. God only blesses what He has ordained. Maybe you know some people who are paying bitterly for something that they ordered and made happen. Maybe he thought he married Ms. America only to discover later that she really is Ms. Jezebel. Or perhaps she thought she married Prince Charming only to be rudely awakened to the fact that he is really a toad.

The enemy is quite skilled at sending counterfeits to us before the right one comes along, and he attempts to trick us into settling for someone other than the one God has for us. We need to be very cautious because the enemy doesn't want us to have God's best. If he can get us to settle for any good Christian person, or even a very nice, good-looking and successful non-Christian, then he wins and we lose.

It is so easy to fall into that trap, especially for those who have had bad relationships in the past. Often they are just so glad and thankful that finally someone took notice. Relieved that they are no longer seen as "damaged goods," they blindly and carelessly fall into the same trap again without even bothering to guard their hearts or seek confirmation, prayer, accountability, and counseling from spiritually strong and discerning people, including leaders.

If you have been blinded before, make yourself accountable! Place yourself under a spiritual covering where trusted spiritual leaders can speak into your life. Trust them more than you trust yourself. Don't set yourself up for another bad experience. Ignorance is making a mistake the first time for lack of knowing better. Stupidity is making the same mistake over and over and never learning from it.

Many singles make the mistake of limiting their source of confirmation, guidance, wisdom, and discernment to their own circle of friends. While friends generally have the best of intentions, their counsel can easily be misguided because their judgment is biased by their affection for you. Because your friends want to see you happy and because they accept your word that marriage will make you happy, they tend to approve of anyone you choose who seems good enough. Friends tend to judge from the surface without probing deeper. Generally it is wiser to seek counsel, discernment, and wisdom regarding a potential partner from trusted spiritual leaders who are spiritually mature because they are more able to make sound judgments.

> *Drink water from your own well—share your love only with your wife. Why spill the water of your springs in public, having sex with just anyone? You should reserve it for yourselves. Don't share it with strangers. An evil man is held captive by his own sins; they are ropes that catch and hold him. He will die for lack of self-control; he will be lost because of his great foolishness* (Proverbs 5:15-17; 22-23 NLT).

If you developed a desire for the forbidden during your singleness, you will still desire it even after you have married. The forbidden things in life bring bondage to the soul. If you have had that problem in the past, I urge you to get delivered from it quickly so that you can start anew with nothing unholy pulling you the wrong way. It will take humility on your part to admit that you have a problem, that you need other people to help you be totally delivered and set free from those chains. Accountability is crucial. Be encouraged, because God gives grace to the humble but resists the proud (see Prov. 3:34).

Mr. "Counterfake"

When I was in my teens, our church hired a new youth pastor. He and his wife were graduates of Christ for the Nations Bible Institute in Dallas, Texas, and they brought new life into our youth group. Full of life and the anointing of the Spirit, they impacted my life in reaching out to other young people. I was drawn to them because of their love and passion for God and because of their music. After high school, I began helping with the youth as a youth leader. I was also the only young person who was committed to praying for the church, and over time I became a faithful intercessor.

One summer, two young guys from the same Bible school came to do their internship at our church, helping with the youth. Since I was a youth leader, I worked closely with both of them. They were full of passion for the youth and did an excellent job firing them up. They even did some miming in the streets. The kids had awesome experiences and encounters with the Lord. On the surface everything looked great.

The summer went well, except for one problem. Both of those guys started liking me. One was slightly older while the other was closer to my age. The last two weeks of their stay, I ceded to my emotions. Actually, I was drawn more to the younger one's anointing and charisma and the way he related to the youth. We shared the same vision, passion, and fire for the Lord. Like any "humanistic" Christian, I noticed how much we had in common, plus the opportunity that we had to get to know each other better and work together. From there, it was easy to calculate the logic of it all and go with the "flow." This is where most people make their biggest mistake and allow circumstances to guide them into relationships that God never truly ordained.

Surely it was God who brought them to my church. But it wasn't

God's plan for them to let their emotions get in the way of their ministry. It should have been a "don't mix business with pleasure" kind of relationship. We should have left it at that level and maintained a very controlled friendship, with God as the focus. Unfortunately, toward the very end, I gave in to my emotions and allowed this one guy's charisma and persistence to get to me. I was still very careful how I went about it, so we were in more of a "friendship-dating" kind of relationship. I was somewhat blinded by his anointing, but I never really saw him for who he was apart from it. There was no physical contact at all, not even holding hands. We simply did a lot of talking and walking together and shared certain experiences about God. Nothing "mushy" happened.

I immediately told my family and church leaders about our relationship. I had developed a deep dislike for secrecy. As much as possible, I was an open book and did not hide anything, especially from my family or church leadership. I learned that whatever is hidden is in darkness and that the enemy is always in the darkness. I refused to have that in my life. This guy had dinner several times with my whole family, and things seemed to be going well. Everybody liked him so far.

The time came when we had to be physically separated. He had to go back to Bible school and finish his last semester. I was still attending the local university. But we continued writing and calling each other. I still needed to get to know him as his own person and not as a co-laborer in the ministry, which was all that I knew about him so far. We started dating only two weeks prior to his departure.

THE TRUTH UNVEILED

During this time of separation, I got more involved in my church and daily went there to pray at six in the morning. I made a commitment to God to be an intercessor and to pray also about my future and the relationship that I had with this guy. God knew that my heart was after Him and His will for my life, so when I asked Him to show me who this guy really was as a person, He did. I kept telling Him that I only wanted His perfect will for my life and nothing else. So my eyes were opened to the truth, and so were my ears.

The more that he wrote me about how he was doing in school, the more I got to know him. Apparently I was his first "girlfriend." Issues of insecurity and immaturity came through his letters, which bothered me a great deal. Apart from the anointing, I was over-whelmed by things in him that turned me off completely. I've always liked athletes, and although he played basketball, he did not quite fit what I wanted—someone who was tall and muscular. However, what annoyed me the most was the way he constantly tried to make me jealous by talking about other girls.

I have no doubt that this guy loved God and had a powerful anointing, especially when he did mime, but he definitely was not my perfect match. I couldn't picture myself babysitting my husband and putting up with all of his insecurities. I thank God for opening my eyes to the truth, and I am forever grateful for it, as is my dear husband, David.

The First Time I Saw His Face

In the middle of the fall semester of my second year in college, God led me to check out Christ for the Nations Bible Institute during a little school break. In the past, right after high school, I had checked out other Bible schools, mainly Assembly of God schools, but I didn't feel led to attend any of them. This one was different. Since my boyfriend was still around, finishing his last semester there (we were still dating long-distance), he was going to show me around when I got there.

The day before I left home, all day long I heard references to the story of Ruth and Naomi on the Christian radio. The last song that was sung before I went to bed was based on the very verse that the Lord had given me in Ruth for my future husband. My logical side started telling me that maybe God was signaling me to give this verse to my boyfriend. I wasn't ecstatic about that idea, but I assumed that that was what God was telling me to do.

I thought maybe God was going to zap him and change him by the time I saw him again. I had foolishly convinced myself that this relationship was from God. So I went with uneasiness in my spirit because I wasn't entirely certain it was right. I didn't have peace in my heart about him. Red flags were going up.

My boyfriend picked me up at the airport, drove me to the campus, and introduced me to all of his friends. The guys were totally eager to meet me while the girls were checking me out to see if I was for real or not. When the two of us were finally alone, I was appalled by his nonchalant behavior toward me, as if he expected me to chase after him or beg for his attention. But I was not that type.

Right before lunch, he called me to meet him at the cafeteria. I went, but didn't find him. So I got my lunch and sat by myself. A student started flirting with me, "Haven't I seen you before? You're from California, right?"

"You must be mistaking me for someone else, because I'm from Chicago," I said. At that moment a tall, buff, and handsome angel came from nowhere and rescued me by asking me to join his table where he was eating with his friends. I quickly accepted. This handsome angel was David Herzog.

As we ate, he began sharing his testimony and how he ended up in Bible school. It was strange, because the more I listened to him, the more his life and walk with God resembled mine. Something inside of me was being stirred. I thought that it was just the excitement of hearing someone else's testimony, but it wasn't. In return, I shared a little bit about myself with David and his friends. I told them that I had two years left before getting my college degree and that afterward perhaps God would allow me to go to this Bible school. Deep inside I was thinking, *This is quite some guy. There is something very different and special about him that interests me. Why then am I stuck with this immature and insecure jerk? Is God punishing me for something?*

After a little while, David and his friends had to go, so I was left alone at the table. I was almost finished with my food when my boyfriend finally arrived. I asked him where he had been and what had taken him so long. He said very nonchalantly that he had been in his room and that he hadn't felt the need to rush down and eat.

As I now see it now, I believe God allowed this to happen so that I could meet David and so that I could see my boyfriend for how he truly was.

I made the mistake of telling my boyfriend about the verses in Ruth that God had given me for my future husband. It happened while we were downtown having dinner. He was so happy with what I told him that, for the first time, he decided to hold my hand, explaining that it meant so much to him because it signified two people being intertwined. Holding hands was a big deal to him; I simply put up with it. Deep inside, though, I was thoroughly confused. Ironically, I saw David with his best friend downtown acting like fools for Jesus. They made me laugh.

After the weekend was over, I flew back home to Chicago.

DAVID'S OBEDIENCE

When I first met David, he was in his first semester of Bible school. God had given him clear instructions not to date anybody during his first semester. In fact, God didn't want him to even go out with his "guy" friends. The only exception was when his best friend from Arizona came to visit him during College Days, around the same time that I visited the school. God wanted David to spend all of his free time alone in his room seeking His face. He willingly obeyed out of his love and devotion to Him. There were times when he would just cry in His presence because of feeling so secluded from everyone, but he knew that God wanted to meet with him every day in that secret place. So he didn't date at all.

When he first met me, he told his best friend that if ever God would let him go out with someone, he would choose me. Apparently, as I shared my testimony, he too had a stirring deep inside. He later told me that there was something very different about me compared to all the other girls that he had met. He said that he saw a certain glow of God's glory on my face that struck him. But when he saw me holding hands with my boyfriend, he was disappointed. He started thinking, *Well, she said she still had two more years before finishing school, and I don't have two more years to waste waiting. I have a mission from God to travel and to win Europe for Jesus. I guess she's not the one for me. Besides, she's already taken.*

Shortly after this, as he was praying in the school's prayer room, a man came up to him and began to prophesy. He said, *Thus says the Lord: because you have obeyed Me and sought Me with all your heart, I am giving you your wife sooner than you think. And she will travel with you wherever you go as you minister together all over the nations.* David simply wrote it all down and put it in his drawer, where he did not look at it again until much later. He believed that, if it was really God, it would happen by itself. If it wasn't, oh well.

At that time, David was so satisfied with the Lord that he wasn't looking for a girlfriend, much less a wife. He was one of those who surrendered to the Lord his right to be married so that he could serve Him with all of his heart, with no distractions. He was willing to be a "bachelor to the rapture" if that was what God wanted for him. The Lord knew that he wasn't at all made or called to be single forever, and He wanted him to be married one day. But it touched God that David was willing to give up marriage for Him.

THE "NORMAL" YOU

It would be wise to take an honest look and do a thorough evaluation of yourself. If you truly are not ready and prepared for marriage spiritually, emotionally, mentally, vocationally, and financially, why encourage another person to need and want you and oblige him or her to meet your emotional, physical, and even spiritual needs? By looking to another person to satisfy your needs, you are telling God indirectly that you don't trust Him to take care of you or to have your best interests at heart. Only God can meet and fulfill those needs.

If you present yourself as spiritually strong in order to impress another person, but apart from that person you are not at all fired up for God, then all you're doing is putting on a show and deceiving that other person with the hope of being pursued as a potential marriage partner. If you change your behavior merely to win the other person's heart and approval, you are cheating that person and putting on a pretense. The motive of your heart is wrong. God sees and knows this, and He cannot bless it.

Here's the true test: will you still behave the same way if God tells you to cut off your current relationship and leaves you uncertain of what the future may hold? Will you still keep the same high standards, or will you go back to the way you were before? This is the only way to really know your own heart and your true motive for doing and behaving differently from your "normal" self.

We only cheat ourselves when we deceive others about who we really are. Marriage will change that in a heartbeat because it is one place where you cannot hide your true self. You have to be ready to be totally exposed for who you really are, and that's a vulnerable place to be. It's not a place for actors, unless you want to do like the actors, who divorce their spouses as soon as they can't keep up the "act" any longer.

Just because someone is a Christian and shares your beliefs doesn't make him or her the right one or God's best choice for you. That's what I thought when I was with my boyfriend, until the Lord enlightened me. But I had to truly seek Him out, and it was to my advantage that there was distance between us at that time, which allowed me to hear God better and to see things more clearly. I had to get beyond the humanistic and superficial way of thinking. Don't let yourself fall into that trap.

I learned that it's better to hear from God when you're not in a relationship than when you're already in one; otherwise your emotions and desires toward the other person are already in play, easily drowning out God's voice. In my situation, the distance between us, the friendship level we kept without physical closeness, the very little and safe "alone time" we had, my serious walk with God, and my true desire to please Him and do what was right all allowed me to hear God clearly concerning this person. In the end, my cautiousness and high standards—not to mention God's revelation—saved me. Hallelujah!

I believe that there is only one perfect match for each of us. One can't open a door with the wrong key, no matter how much it resembles the right one. In the same way, there are not ten different people who can qualify to be God's best for you. Only the right one qualifies.

Wait on the Lord. Rest in Him, and trust Him to bring the two of you together at the right time. Most likely He will do it when you're not looking for anyone, when you're completely satisfied as a single person, when your intimacy with God is all that fulfills you. He will make it happen without any effort on your part. Let go of that desire, and let God have His way with you. All you have to do is wait in His presence and relax. Let Him handle your whole life and future. He will never disappoint you.

chapter 11

MY LOVE STORY

A week after visiting the Bible school, I had a strange dream. I dreamt that I was back there and that, everywhere I went, David was there with me. When I woke up, I thought that maybe the dream was from the pizza I had eaten the night before. You never know what kind of dreams you will have after eating one of those big, thick, juicy Chicago pizzas! So I didn't think anymore about it. I didn't even think of David after that.

Here's the strange thing, though. When I got back to school, it was time to pre-register for the next semester, and the Lord told me not to do it. I knew that my dad was not going to like it, so I said nothing to him for awhile. However, I continued praying at church at six every morning. I never missed a day.

I began fasting for my calling and concerning my relationship with my boyfriend. I wanted to make sure that he was God's choice for me, so I shared my feelings about him with the youth pastor's wife. She knew him to be quite immature but not to the degree that I shared. She said that God loved me so much that He was revealing his faults to me. I totally agreed. The more I sought God about him, the less peace I felt.

One day, as I was on my face in prayer with the other intercessors, the Lord spoke to me. He said clearly, *Stephanie, drop everything and go to Bible school. I want you to go there next semester and forget all about your college degree. I have greater things in store for you. You won't need to go to school to see people healed. You'll see them healed miraculously through your hands.* I didn't question what He said; just like Mary (see Luke 1:30-38), I simply asked how it was going to happen, knowing that my dad would be completely against it. He replied, *I'll take care of everything. Just go!* You can't argue with the Boss. I quickly shared this with the other intercessors before we closed in prayer. Amazingly, they all bore witness with me and received in their spirits that it was truly the Lord telling me this. They continued to pray for me.

I quickly told my mom everything. She knew it was God and told me how she had seen the call of God on my life, even while I was a young child. She never doubted it. She agreed to pray for me about it. We decided to share it with our pastor. He confirmed it too, as he had seen my faithfulness in church. Not only that, but he also possessed wisdom in how to break the news to my dad. He told me to make an appointment with my parents to see him. He would do all the talking and convincing. I agreed and did as he said.

CUTTING THE UMBILICAL CORD

All four of us were in a meeting room, and my pastor began sharing that he saw God's call on my life and that God was calling me to go to Bible school very soon. My dad listened and then asked, "Why does she have to go to that one? There are many Bible schools in Chicago. She doesn't have to go far away just to do that." My pastor explained that God was calling me to that specific school and asked if my dad would give me a year to try it and see from there. If it didn't work out, I could always come back and continue the rest of my studies in Chicago.

Then my dad hesitantly said, "OK, but since God is the One telling her to go there, let Him pay for it then. She's not going to get anything from me, not one penny. Only if she continues her studies here will I pay for her education and anything else she wants; otherwise she's on her own."

I reminded my dad that I had been obedient to him all of my life but that this time I had to obey God above him. I was happy that I could go. Only now God had to come up with the money. And I knew that He pays for what He orders.

My dad set his mind to make it impossible for me to go. The first thing that he did was sell the car that he had bought me, and he kept the money so that I could not use it to go to Bible school. He refused to buy me an airline ticket. He kept insisting that God should pay for it. I fasted like I'd never done before. For a full week, I fasted for all my finances and transportation. Then my pastor felt led to have a special offering for me in church for those who would want to participate in helping pay for my Bible training. My mom started keeping money aside behind my dad's back to help me as well. My friends threw a "farewell party" for me at my house (while my dad was gone), and they decided to pass a hat around to help pay for my school. Altogether, I had 75 percent of my tuition. All I needed was transportation to get there and a couple hundred dollars more, and I would be all set.

One day an unusual boldness came over my mom; she stood up to my dad and said, "I have my own car, and I can do whatever I want with it. So I have decided to take Stephanie to Bible school, and no one's stopping me." My dad was speechless at Mom's determination. It was completely unlike my mom to stand up strong like that—she has more of a lamb-like personality. But something supernatural came over her, and nothing was going to stop her. My dad tuned up her car, checked the tires, and made sure that everything was in perfect condition before we left in late December.

Incidentally, from the day that I left Chicago to go to Bible school, my father refused to ever speak to me again. He practically disowned me for pursuing my call instead of a college degree. He had high hopes for me and was sorely disappointed at my decision. To him, being a minister meant begging for money instead of making money. He couldn't accept that and thought of it as something shameful or as settling for something lower than working in a professional field.

When I decided to follow Christ, it meant leaving everything behind and never looking back. It was difficult and painful, but I had to do it. I had to carry my cross and follow Him, even if it meant breaking my father's heart. I had to cut the umbilical cord and lose my life in order to gain it back from the Lord in another way.

Two men from the church, who were part of the intercessory group, offered to take turns driving my mom's car because they didn't want her to drive such a long distance back home all alone, especially during winter. Chicago was covered with snow at the time, and the route to Dallas would be treacherous. A girl friend of mine also decided to come along to see me off. I thank God for sending people my way to help me, even to the very last detail.

On the way to Dallas, my mom wanted to stop in Oklahoma to visit her cousin and his family. They were Christians, and they gave me money for school because they were touched by my testimony. God is so faithful! Ours is a God of more than enough, not barely enough or just enough! By the time I reached Christ for the Nations Bible Institute, I had more than enough money for all that I needed, plus an extra couple hundred dollars with which to open a bank account. God really did pay for everything! This became the beginning of me walking and living by faith. He has never failed me. I knew I could always trust Him. No matter how impossible things may seem, my Father is bigger and greater.

BREAKING UP WAS A JOY

Therefore, since we are surrounded by such a huge crowd of witnesses to the life of faith, let us strip off every weight that slows us down, especially the sin that so easily hinders our progress. And let us run with endurance the race that God has set before us (Hebrews 12:1 NLT).

I arrived in Dallas a week before school started. My boyfriend was excited that I was attending school there, and he planned to live on campus even though he had already graduated. Nothing had changed with him, and I had had enough. I told my roommates about my problem, and one of them suggested that I break up with him. What a great idea! No one had ever said that, not even the leaders of my church. I don't know why I never thought of it. I guess I was deceived into thinking that somehow I was stuck with him.

When God gives us His best, they will not be someone we have to "put up with" or "settle for." So I did what Hebrews 12:1 tells me to do—*"strip off every weight that slows me down."* The words *break up* were so liberating to me that I quickly arranged to meet him the very next night in front of my dorm. I simply told him everything and didn't leave out even the tiniest detail. For me, it was all over. After I broke up with him, I felt so free and so happy. But that night, before I went to sleep, I was bothered by the fact that I would be seeing him around campus. I wanted to be able to forget about him. I asked the Lord to erase supernaturally all of my memories of him and to break off every soul tie.

That night I saw him in my dream, but couldn't for the life of me remember his name. I kept saying the wrong names. I became so frustrated because I kept saying that I knew this guy from somewhere; I just couldn't remember his name. Finally, I woke up and looked for a picture of him with his name on the back. That was the only way that I remembered who he was. God did what I had asked. So I tore up and threw away all of his pictures and letters. There was no use keeping them. I was a new and free woman!

I told God that I didn't want a boyfriend while I was in school.

I was completely satisfied with just Him and me. I yearned for it to stay that way for a long time. I hadn't sacrificed and left everything behind just to play around. I was there for serious business—to prepare myself for His call and then do it. I had no time to waste and get distracted.

TOGETHER WITH POWER

On the very first day of school, I bumped into David. He was in total shock when he saw me! The first thing he asked me was what happened with my college degree. He remembered our first meeting and that I had two more years to go. I simply told him that God had better plans for me, so there I was. David was very happy to see me. When he asked about my boyfriend, I informed him that the relationship was over. At the time, I honestly did not think much about David, nor did I have any interest in getting any closer. I meant business with God, keeping in mind the words from Proverbs:

Guard your heart above all else for it determines the course of your life. Look straight ahead, and fix your eyes on what lies before you. Mark out a straight path for your feet; stay on the safe path. Don't get sidetracked; keep your feet from following evil (Proverbs 4:23; 4:25-27 NLT).

I did all of that. In order to have the grace and the strength to do that diligently, one has to spend a lot of intimate time with the Lord. Only from spending much time in the secret place (the prayer closet) with God do we become so full of Him that we do not want or need anything or anyone else. When our cup is always full of Him, there is no room or desire for other things.

Oddly enough, David and I were in the same classes. We bumped into each other every day. Whenever I was looking for a seat, the one next to him would be the only one open. But I guarded myself. Each time we found ourselves together just to chat while in the front foyer of the auditorium, in the hallway, or the cafeteria, we always talked about the Lord and the wonderful things He did. We would fire each other up. I was able to share with him the vision God had given me for France and Europe.

Amazingly, David told me that he too had received a similar vision from the Lord even before coming to Bible school. How strange that was! The other bizarre thing was that, whenever we were together, someone always seemed to get saved, healed, or delivered. We both felt the compulsion of faith and power to put what we learned into practice quickly, instead of keeping it as head knowledge, and we saw immediate results. It was amazing! We did street evangelism together in different places with our school. We evangelized in places where satanists hung out, in gay bars, etc. The presence of all that sin neither appalled nor intimidated us. We had such a love for the sinners and wanted to bring them hope and a new life in Christ. One thing's for sure, we were never bored in Bible school!

Then there was the Mardi Gras outreach that I felt led by the Lord to join. I saw David again at the hall where we gathered. The leader divided all of us up in pairs. David ended up as my partner. Our schedule called for us to pray a few hours a day with our group and our partners and to fast in preparation for the outreach, which promised to be intense. The leader suggested also that we prepare ourselves physically by working out at the gym because we would be doing a lot of walking. By the time the outreach event arrived, we were prepared, spirit, soul, and body. We were ready for battle. Again, powerful things happened whenever we were together.

WHO'S TALKING TO ME?

One day, as I was praying alone, I heard a voice tell me that David was going to be my husband. My immediate response was, "I bind that thought in Jesus' name!" Each time I heard it, I bound it automatically and, after a while, almost with anger, because the thought bugged me constantly. I really thought it was the devil trying to distract me. I kept on rebuking it. After hearing it many times, I finally said to God, *Lord, I'm sick and tired of hearing this. I'm willing even to cut off my friendship with this guy if that's what it takes for this to stop. I'm serious about no dating, no distractions!*

But it only got worse. This time, it seemed that wherever I went David was always there. I would go to the bookstore; he would be there. I would go to the library; he would be there too. Even when I went to work out in the gym, he was already there. My roommate would watch him work out, and drool over him. Once when she teased me to go out with him, I responded firmly, "Why don't you go out with him? You're the one who's drooling over him. You're the one who likes him. He's just a friend. If you want, I'll fix you up with him." I truly was serious about not dating anyone. But my friend chickened out.

Finally, I got mad at God and said, *Lord, what is happening here? You were supposed to keep him away from me. But instead he is always exactly where I happen to be. Why are you not answering my prayers? Why is the opposite happening here instead? I don't understand.*

The Lord patiently waited until I was finished. Finally He said, *Well, first of all, will you stop binding and rebuking? It's not the devil who has been talking to you and crossing your paths together. It's been Me all this time. I'm the One who is putting you two together.*

I was shocked and had to take a deep breath. *What did You just say God? It's been You all this time? No way! But I'm not asking for a husband now. I don't need one right now, and I don't want one right now. I'm perfectly satisfied with just You and me.*

He replied, *But I want to put you two together now because I believe you both are ready, and I have great things for you two to do for My Kingdom.*

I quickly responded, *Your Word says to test everything. Well, I will put this to test. If it's really You telling me this, I want a myriad of genuine confirmations from spiritually discerning and mature people who know nothing about anything concerning this. And David should be receiving this same information from You too. Then I'll believe it's truly You doing this. I'd better get my mom in on this. I'll ask her to fast and pray about this too.*

I told my mom, and she promised to fast and pray. As soon as she received anything from the Lord, she would tell me.

BINDING AND REBUKING

At that time, I was not aware of what was happening with David. He told me later that he too started hearing a voice telling him that I was going to be his future wife. His immediate response was the same as mine. He began binding and rebuking the devil because he was not going to date anyone. He was guarding his heart as well.

Actually, both of us were resisting. Even though David and I had the same fire for God and the same call and vision from God, we were still not convinced it was God. Those things are very important things to have in common of course. You can't marry someone called to India when God has called you to Peru. God will make sure that you are a perfect match, with the same spirit and calling. God is the key ingredient. All of the other ingredients can be present, but without God initiating and leading, and many genuine, proven, and tried confirmations, then it is not from Him. If He's not in the pie, don't you dare eat it, even though it outwardly looks good and enticing. That pie is not meant for you. It's meant for someone else, and if you choose to eat it, you're eating someone else's pie. Get the picture?

When it's truly God putting two people together, you never have to make it happen. He does it all and doesn't need your help. Also, you'll never miss it because, even if you resist it like we both did, it will come to pass anyway. After all, it's God who decides if marriage is part of His plan for you, when it should take place, and with whom. So just surrender everything to God and let Him do His thing.

Like me, David kept hearing the same message nonstop, so he finally asked God to confirm it to him through other people who knew nothing about the situation. Shortly after, David and I both received separately more confirmations than we could handle. For example, one guy in David's dorm came up to him one day and said:

"David, take it or leave it, but as I was praying I saw a vision of you having your eyes fixed on God, and parallel to you was a girl God has shown you, and her eyes are also fixed on God. God is above you both and the three of you form a triangle with God as the tip with the two of you on each corner. Because your eyes are not on each other but on God alone, as you keep following Him upward, you two will automatically end up together. If it means something to you, take it as from the Lord."

Then he walked away. This person knew nothing about anything going on between us, so he qualified as one who could give an absolute confirmation about us. And he did. That specific vision impacted David the most.

Later on, my mom called me and told me that she had heard from the Lord while in the bathroom of all places. She heard Him say: *Fear not, for I am the one putting Stephanie and David together for My purposes. I have great things in store for them, and together they shall do great and mighty things for the advancement of My Kingdom. Fear not, and have peace! It is I who speaks it.*

She couldn't have wished for anything clearer than that. And even though she had never met David, my mom had perfect peace about him. She knew him only in the Spirit as she prayed for this whole thing. And since God had chosen him for me, she was totally for it. After word got out, some guys from my home church who liked me asked my mom if she really felt a peace about David. She told them that she did, with absolute confidence.

My mom had complete trust in God and I did too. But I told the Lord, *OK, You were right as always. Your Word says, "The man who finds a wife finds a treasure and receives favor from the Lord"* (Prov. 18:22 NLT). *He had better be the one to initiate. I'm not one to make the first move. He's got to find me, and I'll just stay put until he does. That's my job according to Your Word.*

God granted it. Take note that God says that he who finds a wife (meaning the one from Him, not just any wife that the man may choose) finds a treasure and obtains favor from Him. This means also that the woman doesn't do the finding or the pursuing. That is the man's job. God then reminded me of the verses in Ruth that He had given me long before that related to my future husband. He told me that is was time to give those verses to David to see how they corresponded with what He had already told David about his future wife.

THE MOST-AWAITED MOMENT

One night after dinner, David invited me to join him at the girls' dorm fellowship hall, where we were allowed to have male guests since it was a room with big windows and was monitored by the Resident Assistants. When we sat down, he began to tease me by saying that he loved my hair, then my eyes, and then my smile. I was starting to get irritated because he was just kidding. I wanted to hear what God had showed him, not what he loved about me. Finally, he said that he was falling in love with me, and he began sharing all of the things that God had revealed to him about me.

Then I shared with him the confirmations that I had received and, finally, the verses in Ruth. He was amazed to see how God had matched every detail that we each received separately from Him. Only God could have arranged all of that. God is the One and Only Matchmaker!

And so we concluded finally that we were meant for each other. The questions were: *What do we do now? Were we boyfriend and girlfriend, or fiancés, since it was a commitment to marriage, not just to date or "go steady"?* We decided that we might as well call it what the Bible called it—we were betrothed to each other. We quickly told the leaders of the school, our families, and our home pastors. Once it was settled that this relationship was totally ordained by God from the very beginning with marriage as the goal, we finally began to spend romantic times together.

SUBMISSION TO AUTHORITY

We told our families and presented each other to them. My dad still wouldn't talk to me, so as usual, my mom was the only one who shared this precious moment with me. Everyone we told (apart from my dad) was happy about our relationship. We started submitting our relationship to the leaders of the Bible school and asked for their approval, guidance, and pre-marital counseling. We asked God to use them to give us the wisdom in how to go about the whole marriage issue, particularly regarding the right timing of it.

After a series of intense interviews, our school approved of our engagement. The final stage was deciding when we should get married. They said that sooner than a year would be too quick, but longer than a year would not be good either. So they suggested a date more or less toward the end of my second semester that year. They allowed us to take the "Marriage and Family" class together for the second semester so that, by the time the class was over, we would have learned about our roles in establishing a godly marriage and about how to raise a family in the ministry/mission field effectively.

In addition to the leaders of the school, we also sought pre-marital counseling from married friends we knew at school, our pastors back home, and other spiritual leaders. We even had a weekly pre-marital counseling session with the teacher of our "Marriage and Family" class until the week before we got married. We were the ones who asked for it and sought it out because we wanted to do everything right.

Where no wise guidance is, the people fall, but in the multitude of counselors there is safety.... The way of a fool is right in his own eyes, but he who listens to counsel is wise (Proverbs 11:14; 12:15).

Plans go wrong for lack of advice; many advisers bring success (Proverbs 15:22 NLT).

He who willfully separates and estranges himself [from God and man] seeks his own desire and pretext to break out against all wise and sound judgment. A [self-confident] fool has no delight in understanding but only in revealing his personal opinions and himself.... The mind of the prudent is ever getting knowledge, and the ear of the wise is ever seeking (inquiring for and craving) knowledge (Proverbs 18:1-2,15).

This wisdom applies also to couples. If we were certain that our relationship was God-ordained, there was no reason to fear outside counsel and accountability. They would only confirm, help, and guide us in our relationships. David and I were not avoiding it; on the contrary, we valued it, hungered for it, and sought for it. Those who avoid outside counsel may be uncertain that their relationship is from God. Pride, rebellion, and doubt are the problems.

"There is a way that seems right to a man and appears straight before him, but at the end of it is the way of death" (Prov. 16:25). Although the word *death* here certainly includes physical death, it likely refers more to spiritual death. Following our own way rather than God's always keeps us from fulfilling God's will for our lives. Here is a final encouraging word regarding wise counsel: *"He who deals wisely and heeds [God's] Word and counsel shall find good, and whoever leans on, trusts in, and is confident in the Lord—happy, blessed, and fortunate is he"* (Prov. 16:20).

I can't tell you how happy David and I were when God brought everything together without our getting in the way to manipulate it. The glory is His and His alone. When people try to make it happen on their own, God doesn't get the glory. Wait for God to do it supernaturally.

MY FATHER'S BLESSING

Someone asked David if he had asked for my dad's blessing. He thought about it and realized that he hadn't. That was one thing that we truly wanted from God, so I challenged Him one last time.

I said to Him:

Lord, so far You have been so gracious and granted me every challenge that I've given You to prove that this relationship is from You. But there is one last thing that You need to do for me. I want my dad's approval and blessing concerning marrying David because I believe that the father's blessing is so important in Your Word. I know it looks impossible right now since he won't even talk to me, let alone give me his blessing, but I know that You are well capable of doing the miraculous and making it happen. Please do that miracle for me. I'm asking You, as Your dear daughter, from the very bottom of my heart. This means the world to me.

David and I fasted an entire day for that very purpose. When evening came, we decided to call my dad. I placed the call and he answered. Normally he would pass the phone quickly to my mom to avoid talking to me, but this time he actually talked. (That was not mere coincidence!) He told me that my mom had been updating him with the latest news about me and that he had heard about David. He asked if he could talk to him. He had talked to me for about five minutes and then wanted to talk to David.

I passed the phone to David, and he and my dad talked for at least an hour. I was shocked. He was testing him to see if the man I was going to marry was a smart man and not some dumb jock. He was very impressed with David. They talked about all kinds of things from cars to politics, and David answered all of my dad's questions very well. Right before David was about to ask for my father's blessing, my dad beat him to it. My dad said to David, "I'm glad to be able to talk to you and get to know you a bit. I just wanted to find out what kind of man my daughter is about to marry. If she's happy with you, then I'm happy too. I give you my blessing."

Is God a miracle-working God or not? I told you that God is not a cheapskate and that He gives gifts from above that are perfect and of the highest quality. Never accept or settle for anything less! Wait on the Lord until He gives His perfect plan to you.

chapter 12

HAPPILY EVER AFTER

This final chapter highlights amazing testimonies from people who are being used and who were used mightily by God. Some stories are about married people who share how God supernaturally orchestrated their relationship, very much like how God did with me and David. Others are from singles who are living their lives in complete surrender to God, fulfilling His will in their lives while enjoying life to the fullest.

Their true stories testify that God's plan truly works. Any Christian willing to meet God's conditions can experience the same joy. My prayer is that you chose to be a living epistle, either as a single who's satisfied in God or as a partner in a divinely ordained marriage that is committed to following God's standards and ways.

BEN D'SOUZA

God's principles work despite your race and background. Here is a wonderful testimony from Ben D'Souza who is one of our spiritual sons in the glory in Dubai, United Arab Emirates. Originally from India, Ben is a young, fired-up pastor in Dubai. His story about how God supernaturally put him and his bride, Francesca, together follows:

I gave my life to the Lord in May 2003, as the result of years of prayers from my parents. At the time of my conversion, I was 21 years of age and weighed about 90 pounds. God had set me free from a life filled with drug abuse and depression. I was literally at the end of the road when God turned my life around.

However, my salvation wasn't the only burden my mother had taken up in prayer. She also prayed just as fervently for my future spouse. There were generations of failed marriages in my family, and knowing the danger of generational curses, my mother took the matter up in prayer often to ensure that I would have the kind of marriage that would be a testimony to others. Before I was saved, God had given my mother a promise. He assured her that she would not only have the pleasure of seeing me married to the right person, but that the relationship she would have with her future daughter-in-law would be like that of Ruth and Naomi.

After I got saved, I was consumed with a radical

love for Jesus, even to the point that I didn't care whether I ever married or not. I would gladly have stayed single for the rest of my life knowing that Paul referred to it as a "gift" from God. However, about seven months after my conversion, I was introduced to a girl named Francesca, who would later become my wife. I attended a Sports Day event held by the church, and I was really intrigued from the moment I met her. Although we didn't converse much that day, I hoped to see her again.

As days passed, I found myself constantly thinking about her. I often battled against what I was feeling because I thought it was the enemy trying to entice me and steal me away from Jesus. So I purposely didn't make much contact with Francesca for a month after we met. I needed to know whether these feelings were from God or not. I decided to treat these feelings as though they were not from God until He told me otherwise.

In January 2004, a month after we had met, I was in my room talking to God. The Lord gave me a vision in which I saw what appeared to be a white see-through cloth. I lifted the cloth and saw Francesca's face behind it. I understood immediately that the cloth was a wedding veil. I was excited because I knew what the Lord was telling me. To this day, I remember so clearly the first conversation we had on the telephone because that was when I told her with all the boldness within me, "I'm going to marry you one day!" (Remember, this was the first time we had ever spoken on the phone, but by the grace of God, she didn't hang up on me!) She laughed at what I said, probably because she thought I was trying to be cute.

Francesca started attending the youth group I was a part of because she was hungry to experience what God was doing. We had gone from a group of about 20 to almost 100 in three months. This kind of growth in an Arab, Muslim country is a big deal! Francesca was from a conservative Christian church that didn't believe in the baptism of the Holy Spirit or praying in tongues, but what she saw and experienced made her hungry for more of God. Soon she was baptized in the Holy Spirit while in prayer at her house. Two months later, a prophet from India had a word for her. The prophecy meant a lot to her but even more to me. He said, "The Lord wants you to know, Francesca, that you are as Ruth was in the Bible, and I see that God is going to give you a field, and He will use you to reap His harvest. You will have a small beginning and a big end."

When Francesca related this word to me, I almost jumped out of my skin! I said, "That's the word. That's the confirmation! You're going to be my wife, because the Lord told my mom that she will have a relationship with her daughter-in-law like Ruth and Naomi!" She decided that she wanted to be absolutely sure, so she went into prayer and asked the Lord to confirm it to her in a way that seemed almost impossible. She asked the Lord to send someone to tell her that she was like Ruth, and that the relationship she would have with her mother-in-law would be like that of Ruth and Naomi, and that Naomi's son would be her Boaz! (Those of you who know the story of Ruth from the Bible, know that Naomi's son was not Boaz!) She asked the Lord to confirm it to her in a way that would be a miracle if He did. She hid this from me too and would only tell me that she was waiting for God to confirm it to her.

I wanted to know what the confirmation was that she was looking for. Months passed and I was sure she was to be my wife, but all she kept saying was, "I'm still waiting for God to confirm this!" We were both in love, and we both really wanted to be together forever, but neither one of us was willing to totally commit if God was not for it. So although I had my confirmation, she still needed hers. A whole year passed by, and now it was April 2005. By this time, the Lord had already taught me that I needed to rest in the assurance that all of His promises are yes and amen in Christ Jesus. I didn't need to worry for He would confirm it to her when the time was right.

We were at a friend's house one night for worship. After several hours hanging out in God's glory and soaking, one of the women gave Francesca a prophetic word. This woman hardly knew Francesca. In fact, she had only met her two or three times. There was no way she could have known what Francesca had asked the Lord as confirmation. "Fran," she said, "I believe the Lord wants me to tell you that He has called you to be like Ruth. He's saying that the relationship you will have with your mother-in-law will be like that of Ruth and Naomi and...her son will be your Boaz!" Fran jumped off the floor, crawled right over to me and hugged me with tears in her eyes! I was in shock, not because of the fact that the Lord had confirmed it to her but at the fact the Lord had actually given her the word just as she wanted it!

That was a turning point in our relationship, now

we were absolutely sure, without a shadow of a doubt, that God had brought the two of us together. In December 2006, I took her back to the spot where we first met. We stood on the same stones out in the park in the pouring rain. I got down on one knee and asked her to be my wife. She said, "Yes." Exactly one year later we married. Praise God!

DEREK PRINCE (1915-2003)

Derek Prince was one of God's generals whose life and teachings changed my life. I highly value his anointing and testimony. This man truly lived his life according to God's principles, and the results of such a consecrated life are evident. May his testimony inspire you to hold the same standards. His powerful story follows:

God led me supernaturally to the mate of His choice, and in so doing placed in my hand the key that opened up this mystery. One night in a British Army barrack room, I received a direct personal revelation of Jesus Christ. The next week in the same room, I experienced what I knew to be a supernatural infilling of the Holy Spirit. God suddenly spoke to me words that I never would have thought up myself. What I remember God saying that forever changed my life was simply, *It shall be like a little stream. The little stream shall become a river; the river shall become a great river; the great river shall become a sea; and the sea shall become a mighty ocean...* Somehow I knew those words contained the key to God's purpose for my life.

I had this constant impression that my call was linked somehow with the land and the people of Palestine [as it was called then, later it was changed to Israel]. A fellow Christian soldier who had spent some time in Palestine (Israel) told me of a little children's home there that I must visit if I wanted to receive a real spiritual blessing. A Danish lady ran this children's home. Soldiers went there from all over the Middle East, and God was meeting them in special ways. I never forgot my friend's advice.

Amazingly, I was transferred to Palestine and visited the children's home. The atmosphere was permeated by an invisible presence that settled like dew on men weary from the strain and monotony of desert warfare. The woman in charge was Lydia Christensen who came to Jerusalem from Denmark 16 years before. She started by taking one dying Jewish baby in a basement room, which grew to many children from various racial backgrounds.

Lydia and I agreed to pray about God's plan for me in Palestine as I needed more clarity about it. Simultaneously I began sensing the heavy load and burdens Lydia carried, so I felt led to intercede for her too. Then the Holy Spirit spoke these words to me, *I have joined you two together...under the same yoke and in the same harness...*

At another time, Geoffrey, a Christian soldier friend, blurted out while praying with him, Lord, *You have shown me that that little home will be like a little stream, and the little stream will become a river, and the river will become a great river, and the great river will become a sea...* He repeated word for word exactly what God had said to me about my future. I discovered that God had given Geoffrey—concerning Lydia and the children's home—exactly the same picture of an enlarging stream that He had given me.

I remembered two expressions God had used in Kiriat Motzkin: *Under the same yoke and in the same harness.* A *harness* pictured two animals working together in close relationship. And the *yoke* was a picture used regularly in the Bible of two persons united in marriage. Could that be what God had in mind?

I began to focus on the differences and the difficulties. Lydia was from a cultural background quite unlike mine. She was a strong character, a natural leader. She was used to fighting her own battles. Would she be willing to surrender headship in a home to a man much younger and less experienced than herself? But the positive side was simply that God had spoken. Clearly and supernaturally He had revealed His plan, first of all to me alone. Then through a fellow Christian, He had confirmed it just as clearly and supernaturally. I didn't even pray or desire it. The whole revelation came *solely* from the *sovereign will of God.* If I were to reject God's will so clearly revealed, how could I expect His blessing on my future?

I had excitement at the thought that God had clearly marked-out His plan for my life, yet feared that the task would prove too difficult. I committed myself in faith to the plan He revealed, and allowed Him to work out for me the things I could not work out for myself. So I embraced His plan for me and trusted Him to reveal it in His own way and time.

From this point on, there began an evolving change in my relationship with Lydia. I finally faced the truth that I was in love with Lydia and with the eight children. A few months later, I asked Lydia to marry me, and she said yes. We were married about a month before my discharge in 1946. Later that year we moved to Jerusalem from Ramallah as there was war and famine all around Israel, but God protected and provided for us supernaturally. These experiences as a family created such a unity, bonding us closer than natural families all their life, bonds that still hold today. Our unity was the one major source of strength in our life and ministry that never failed giving us victories that neither of us could ever have gained alone.

A fellow minister once stated, "You two work together just like one person." The more I meditated on Lydia's life after her passing the more I marveled at God's perfect wisdom. She had given God more than fifty years of grueling, selfless service. I had no idea of the kind of life that lay ahead of us while we were married. I had no basis for choosing a wife for myself, since I lacked the vital information on which alone a smart choice could be based. Looking back after thirty years of trials and labors I was overwhelmingly convinced that Lydia was the only woman in the world who could have been a sufficient helper for me through it all. I was amazed not only at how God knew the kind of wife I needed for those many years as He prepared her for me, and how He placed her in the same path, pointing her out to him as the helper He had chosen for me. Each time I go over this in my mind, I bow my head in worship, and say with Paul in Romans 11:33: *Oh, the depth of the riches of the wisdom and knowledge of God! How unsearchable His judgments, and His paths beyond tracing out!*[1]

MATT SORGER

Matt Sorger is a good friend of ours and a single young man whom God is using powerfully to minister healing, salvation, and deliverance to many. His story follows:

Saved at the age of 14, the Lord placed an incredible hunger and thirst in my heart for a true relationship with Him. During my teen years I believe it was my passion for God that kept me from a lot of the pressures of the world around me. In my third year of college, the call of God came strongly upon me. I knew that my life was to be given in complete devotion to God in a vocation of service and ministry. Even before I had this full revelation of God's call, He was already preparing me for it. The Holy Spirit had become my closest friend. I surrendered everything in my spirit, soul, body, and mind to the Lord completely. My greatest passion was to walk with God, share His heart, and live in His presence.

As a result, earthly relationships took a back seat to my relationship with God. I knew, if I were ever to marry, she would need to have the same level of devotion to God and share the same sense of calling for ministry. I take this very seriously. I have made a choice to place all my focus, energy, and attention on God, His will, and His heart. In the process, I am peacefully trusting Him that my days are in His hands. As a man joined to the Lord, I have a deep sense of fulfillment, peace, joy, and contentment that flows out of my relationship with God and from doing His will for my life. My days and times are possessed by the presence of God.

I know life is constantly full of change. I've walked through many different seasons in life and ministry. I live with the revelation that I can enjoy to the fullest each season God has me in. When you are in a season of marriage, you enjoy the company and relationship God gives you with your spouse. But that season comes with its moments of challenge as well. During the season of being "joined to the Lord only," there is a level of communion you experience with God where you are only concerned about one thing—pleasing God and fulfilling His will. Sometimes people pressure me to get married just for the sake of being married. But what they don't understand is that I get to spend all my time with God. Driving in my car, when I am at home, or when I am in my hotel room on the road traveling in ministry, I can spend all my time praying and communing with God. This is a gift!

I can enjoy each day God gives me knowing that at any moment the seasons could shift and God could bring me a wonderful, beautiful, godly woman with whom I can serve God. I'm looking forward to that day as well. But that does not in any way take away from the joy and contentment I have now, nor does it affect the ministry to which God has called me. If anything, it helps me focus more on what God has called me to do. Every moment in my life is given to pursing the advancement of His Kingdom in the lives of those He gives me to minister to. The key is enjoying every day to its fullest and knowing that each season has its own special qualities that are gifts from God.

MATT'S MOTHER, VERONICA

I asked Matt's mom to write something concerning how she prays for her son and handles working with him in full-time ministry as a single. She actually works for her son as his personal assistant. I am so touched and blessed by the beautiful relationship she and her husband have with their son and by how humbly and faithfully they serve him in ministry. Not only do they pray for their son's destiny to be fulfilled, they also believe in him and help him through their selfless service. I've never seen anything like it. It is simply amazing. Here is her testimony:

> Our love and prayers for our children should always reflect the heart of God. God has blessed me with two wonderful sons. I understand the love of God for them, the desire of God's heart to give them the best and to provide a fulfilling and joyful life for each one. It has been and continues to be my prayer that God's will, purpose, and plan for their lives would come to pass. I do not have preconceived ideas of my own, but rather open my heart in faith, interceding for God's Kingdom purposes to come and be manifested in their lives. His plan may include marriage, or it may not. We never want our heart to be in opposition to the heart of the heavenly Father. Let us release our children into God's plan with faith and trust in God and rejoice along with our children as they fulfill their destinies.

RUTH HEFLIN

Ruth Heflin was a spiritual mother to us. Her life and ministry impacted our lives in a very powerful way. She was the one who introduced us to the Glory of God, and our lives and ministry were never the same again. Here is her remarkable testimony of how consecrated her life was to God and the price she paid to be mightily used by God:

As I began serving God in Asia, many powerful things happened. While ministering in Hong Kong, I became engaged to a young man I had known for many years, and we decided to be married in Hong Kong. At first he was to accompany my parents and me on a trip to India right before marrying but the trip did not come together for him. So he encouraged me to go ahead with my parents, and marry upon my return.

We took along all the clothes we needed for the wedding. When I got back to Hong Kong, days passed, then weeks and months, and he still hadn't come. I was torn inside about what God was saying to me. I met with Ed Stube, a known Episcopalian priest from Montana one night. I was about to ask Brother Stube's advice about the confusing feelings I had about getting married when he told me to wait a minute as he felt a prophetic word coming for me.

He suddenly prophesied, *I have called you to ministry around the world. It was not that you doubted My word, but you doubted that I could do it for you. If you will make the consecration, I will prove to you that I am able to do it.* In that moment, I knew that the Lord was requiring me to leave my own desire to marry behind for the ministry. I said nothing to my fiancé at first when, a few days before Christmas, I got a call from him in America saying that he was coming to Hong Kong the next week to marry me.

I started to rationalize that the Lord only wanted me to be willing to give him up. Now that I was willing, I assumed God was going to give me the green light to marry him. I thought that God would give him back to me, as He gave Isaac back to Abraham for being willing. After justifying my decision, I announced to all my friends that I was getting married the next week.

On Christmas morning, I went to church for a holiday service. The pastor spoke on the gold, the frankincense, and the myrrh that the wise men had brought to Jesus. He said that *myrrh represented our willingness to deny ourselves for the sake of the Gospel.* In that moment, the Lord spoke to me very plainly, showing me that when I had said after the prophecy in November that I would give up my fiancé, it was because I did not think he was coming to Hong Kong anyway. God told me, *Now if you gave him to Me, you will be giving Me a gift.* This became my gift to the Lord, and I am still single today.

This decision was not as easy or as clear-cut as it

may sound. Sometime after that, I experienced a battle within, and I was not at all sure that I was doing the right thing. I was vacillating between the will of God and my own will, and I was quite miserable. One night I had a dream. I saw myself in a beautiful house with a lovely mural on the wall. I was holding a beautiful red-haired baby boy in my arms. (My fiancé had red hair.) I heard myself saying, *Everything is wonderful. It couldn't be better. There's only one thing that bothers me, that I can never work for God again.* I was so shaken by the dream that I wrote to my fiancé and told him about my dream, asking him if he would agree for me to continue my ministry?

He wrote back, *How do we know what the future will hold,* hoping he would say, *No matter what the future holds, we will always put God first.* I probably would have considered marriage had he answered differently. I had to obey God and stay single. Although it was one of the most difficult things I ever did, I never once regretted it.

I went on to do great things for God, prophesied to many presidents, and ministered in just about every nation including North Korea. The Lord had given me the key that day when He said, *If you will make the consecration, I will prove to you that I am able to do it.*

Every enlargement of ministry requires a further consecration on our part. As I said yes to God that day, He quickly showed me how He could use me around the world. I knew that He meant it and that *He would remove every obstacle and make a way for me to do His work.* Soon after the following January, I was ministering in India to ten thousand people a night and rejoicing in the miracle of God's grace![2]

MEGAN ALLISON

Megan has been working for us since 2001. We've seen how she's grown in the Lord over the years. She is now being mightily used by God and touching many lives through her work in the production of our television show, "The Glory Zone" and her work in many aspects of our ministry. Her single-and-satisfied testimony follows:

While growing up, my main source of advice about dating and marriage came from Hollywood. *Friends* and *90210* were my examples for how relationships should be. It wasn't until my first year of college that I seriously gave everything over to Jesus and my life changed completely. I felt the presence of God come into my dorm room, change me, and fill me with a divine hunger to know Him. I am so grateful to God for the hunger He gave me as a new Christian. It saved me from a lot of pitfalls. I started to see a lot of things in the "Christian world," especially concerning relationships, that didn't look any different from the world I came out of. Although a bit more innocent on the outside, the same flirting, dating around, trying out girlfriends/boyfriends that I saw in the world were also happening among Christians. Something in me knew that there was something better.

One day when I was spending time in His presence, God told me not to date, not even to go out as friends with my male friends, because He wanted me to spend my time with Him and not get distracted with anyone else. He showed me how His heart as a Father was to protect His daughters and how, just as in Bible times, He is also to be the One to select for His daughters someone made just for them. He also showed me His heart of jealousy for His Bride, an undistracted Bride who has willingly chosen to set her eyes on one Man, and one Man alone—Him.

When I met Stephanie and David many years ago and heard their story of how God called them apart to a life of devotion to Him and how ultimately God sovereignly and supernaturally brought about their union, I noticed many similarities to the things that God had said to me about singleness and marriage.

Their story confirmed to me that God has an ageless standard, which He instigated from the start. It is the best way for each and every one of His children. God wants us to find our peace, fulfillment, and contentment in Him. When He desires it, He will put us with the mate He has prepared for us.

Knowing that I'm single, people sometimes say to me, "Oh, you must be lonely." The reality is, God has promised to place the lonely in families (see Ps. 68:6a). *Single does not mean alone.* God's intention is to place us in families, whether it is a traditional family or a church family. As long as you take your eyes off yourself, you'll start to see that God has placed others around you to be a support to you and you to them.

It has been ten years since the first time I heard Him speak to me and call me to a life set apart for Him. They have been the most amazing, exciting, fulfilling years I have ever experienced. Nothing, not husband or children, can fulfill you like spending time with Him and walking in the things He has called you to do. If that part isn't right in your life, then nothing else you try will ever fulfill you. He is constantly showing me new facets of Himself and His ability to be everything to me, my Father, my

Friend, my Teacher, even my Husband. I mean ultimately, He is the One we as believers are called to be a Bride to anyway. Why not start now?

You now have a chance to rewrite your life. Let go of your disappointments, hurts, and feelings of failure; release them all to God and have total closure. Let go and let God. Step forward into the future that God has for you, knowing that there is nothing that you can do to change your past but that you can certainly change your present and future. Where you are going is more crucial than where you have been. Today is a new day!

Dear brothers and sisters, I am still not all I should be, but I am focusing all my energies on this one thing: Forgetting the past and looking forward to what lies ahead, I strain to reach the end of the race and receive the prize for which God, through Christ Jesus, is calling us up to heaven. But we must be sure to obey the truth we have learned already...Pattern your lives after mine, and learn from those who follow our example (Philippians 3:13-14, 16-17 NLT).

Before you close this book, I challenge you to think about this: if you were to write your very own epistle, what would it say? God's love and grace are yours to help you choose His way. May my life inspire and compel you to trust God with your life and to do things His way. You will quickly see the rewards and the blessings that come with His perfect plan.

Renounce dating. Choose today to find your wholeness,

satisfaction, and fulfillment in God alone. Let Him heal every place you hurt; forgive and release to Him those who have hurt you. Live your life according to God's principles and ways, and you will be greatly blessed. If marriage is part of His plan for you, then rest in God and let Him make it happen supernaturally. If not, let your life be totally dedicated to Him. Live to serve Him and to be a blessing to others in your singleness.

ENDNOTES

1. For the entire story read Derek Prince's *God Is a Matchmaker*. Derek Prince, *God Is a Matchmaker* (Royal Oaks, MI: Chosen Books, 1986).

2. Ruth Ward Heflin, *Harvest Glory* (Hagerstown, MD: McDougal Publishing Company, 1999).

PARTNER WITH US

Supporting the greater cause of reaching the harvest of souls worldwide connects you to a glory and breakthrough greater than what you can accomplish on your own. Together we can accomplish many times more for the Kingdom of God because, for each soul saved, healed, delivered, and transformed in our ministry, you too will receive the same reward from the Lord by partnering with us monthly.

Partners allow us to accomplish beyond what we could do with just our own strength, gifts, and finances. Our ministry travels worldwide, reaching the lost through crusades, outreaches, and feeding the poor, as well as through our television program, "The Glory Zone," which airs nationwide and in every continent. We also faithfully support Israel by giving generously to ministries that feed the poor and help soldiers and terrorist victims and by holding our yearly tour to the Holy Land.

We invite you to be part of "The Glory Zone" family and to enter into the shared blessings of partnering with us to take the Gospel to every nation, tribe, and tongue. Our television program is currently bringing in many souls and opening doors to hold revival meetings and crusades, even in hard-to-enter countries. As you pray and give faithfully to this ministry, we believe that you are sowing into "good" ground—for each seed you sow, you will reap a multiple harvest of souls, and you shall receive impartation as you become partakers of the same grace, favor, and anointing that are in our lives and ministry (see Acts 4).

For each breakthrough in which you help us reach the nations for God through your giving and prayers, He will accelerate and multiply blessings and breakthroughs back into your life. That's what's great about partnership. Please consider partnering with a monthly donation or a large one-time gift to spread the Kingdom of God worldwide and be eternally blessed.

INVITING STEPHANIE HERZOG
TO YOUR AREA

Stephanie Herzog may be available to speak at your church, conference, or special event. Please contact us with the details of your invitation and the nature of the event. Stephanie and her team will pray about your invitation and respond to you as soon as possible.

To become a partner, contact her at:
David Herzog Ministries
Attention: Stephanie Herzog
PO Box 2070
Sedona, AZ 86339

Website: http://www.thegloryzone.org

Check our Website for the schedule of our weekly television program, "The Glory Zone." Also you will see Stephanie and David's itinerary, information on new products, and news about upcoming events, meetings, outreaches, and crusades. Sign up for your free weekly e-mail news and info.

STEPHANIE'S PRODUCTS

DVDs or CDs

We are Supernatural Beings

The School of Miracles

The Weapons of Glory

Experiencing the Supernatural

Living the Supernatural Life

Glory in the Home

Order online at **www.thegloryzone.org,**
or write to **PO Box 2070, Sedona, AZ 86339.**

Additional copies of this book and other
book titles from DESTINY IMAGE are
available at your local bookstore.

Call toll-free: 1-800-722-6774.

Send a request for a catalog to:

Destiny Image® Publishers, Inc.

P.O. Box 310
Shippensburg, PA 17257-0310

*"Speaking to the Purposes of God for this
Generation and for the Generations to Come."*

For a complete list of our titles,
visit us at www.destinyimage.com.